DEBORAH BRUCE

Deborah Bruce is a playw. _
plays include *Godchild* at Hampstead Theatre, *Same* for the
National Theatre Connections Festival 2014, and *The Distance*
at the Orange Tree Theatre and Sheffield Crucible. *The Distance*
was a finalist for the 2012–13 Susan Smith Blackburn Prize.

Deborah Bruce

THE HOUSE THEY GREW UP IN

NICK HERN BOOKS

London

www.nickhernbooks.co.uk

A Nick Hern Book

The House They Grew Up In first published in Great Britain in 2017 as a paperback original by Nick Hern Books Limited, The Glasshouse, 49a Goldhawk Road, London W12 8QP

The House They Grew Up In copyright © 2017 Deborah Bruce

Deborah Bruce has asserted her moral right to be identified as the author of this work

Cover image: Shutterstock/spiber.de

Designed and typeset by Nick Hern Books, London
Printed in the UK by Mimeo Ltd, Huntingdon, Cambridgeshire PE29 6XX

A CIP catalogue record for this book is available from the British Library

ISBN 978 1 84842 643 6

The House They Grew Up In was first produced at Chichester Festival Theatre in a co-production with Headlong on 14 July 2017. The cast, in order of appearance, was as follows:

PEPPY	Samantha Spiro
DANIEL	Daniel Ryan
BEN	Leonardo Dickens/
	Rudi Millard
PC AMANDA GORDON	Michelle Greenidge
SERGEANT HIBBERT	Matt Sutton
SOPHIE	Mary Stockley
DETECTIVE NICHOLS	Matt Sutton
GARETH	Philip Wright
JODY	Daisy Fairclough
KAREN PARRY	Michelle Greenidge
LAURENCE PARRY	Philip Wright
Director	Jeremy Herrin
Designer	Max Jones
Lighting Designer	Natasha Chivers
Music	Paul Englishby
Sound Designer	Emma Laxton
Casting Director	Anne McNulty CDG
Casting Director	Charlotte Sutton CDG

Characters

DANIEL *is very large. He is early forties. He has long hair at the back and sides but very little on the top. He has a beard. He wears a tight yellow T-shirt tucked into suit trousers. He has braces. He has an important watch. He has a big rucksack on his back at all times. He does everything very slowly. He looks like a medieval prophet.*

PEPPY *is a little older than Daniel. She has unbrushed hair, a thick woollen man's jumper, a long skirt and ankle socks and trainers. She speaks very anxiously and continuously. Her tone is not berating or harsh. She is a constant monologue, she has an active, educated mind.*

BEN, *eight years old and lives next door*
SOPHIE, *Ben's mother, mid-thirties*
PC AMANDA GORDON, *a newly trained police constable*
POLICE SERGEANT STEVEN HIBBERT
DETECTIVE CONSTABLE NICHOLS, *male, plain clothes*
GARETH, *a neighbour*
JODY, *a photographer at a local paper*
KAREN PARRY, *a support worker*
LAURENCE PARRY, *Karen's husband*

The Set

The interiors of Nos. 21 and 23 on a Victorian terraced street in South East London.

The kitchen/living room of No. 23.

Peppy is a hoarder. The house is full of their lives' belongings, nothing has ever been thrown away. Boxes, teetering piles of clothes, papers, books, slides, plastic bags full and tied. Movement is only possible through narrow pathways, all surfaces are full and what was once a functioning furnished room is buried.

In contrast, the kitchen at No. 21 is clear and smart and freshly, tastefully designed.

With thanks to Emma Aynsley, Sebastian Born, Daniel Evans, Jeremy Herrin.

D.B.

This text went to press before the end of rehearsals and so may differ slightly from the play as performed.

ACT ONE

Scene One

DANIEL *is alone in the kitchen/living room of No. 23. He is sitting in an armchair listening to music on enormous red headphones. The headphones are connected to a tape player perched on a small stool beside him.*

After a while, PEPPY *comes through the front door and into the room. She has a coat and hat on and a wheelie trolley.*

She comes in, and goes to the tap and turns it on. It trickles weakly.

PEPPY. Still! Oh dear.

> *She takes off her hat and coat. She is perturbed.*
>
> *She looks at* DANIEL. *She goes over and gently lifts off his headphones.*
>
> Hello!
>
> DANIEL *presses stop on the tape player.*
>
> Hello, Daniel.

DANIEL. Hello.

> *Pause.*

PEPPY. Did you turn the tap, did you see how thin the water is, Daniel? It's still the thin water, Daniel, it hasn't come back how it was. I think we need to get a, I think we need to call someone, I don't know who! Do you know who to call, Daniel, about the water being thin? You don't know! Of course you don't! Oh dear, I don't think this is right, I think it's a sign of something, something, really not good with the tap.

> PEPPY *takes off her coat. She carries it around as if she is surprised to find there is no obvious place to put it down.*

After a while she lays it over some piles of things. She considers removing her hat. She leaves it on.

She looks at her watch. She picks up a saucepan.

I waited for half an hour and there was no bus, can you believe it, and then a lady said, there was no bus coming, so I walked to the shops. All the way, Daniel.

DANIEL. What lady?

PEPPY. A lady, Daniel. We don't know her, we've never seen her before. She had a child and a dog. She's just a lady with a child and a dog that we don't know and she told me there was no bus and I walked all the way into town.

DANIEL. Did she have a coat with fur on it?

PEPPY ignores him and squeezes past some things with the saucepan, looking for somewhere to put it down.

PEPPY (*to herself*). All the way into town, all the way home. I don't know why!

Nevermind.

DANIEL. Did she have a coat with fur on it?

PEPPY. No.

DANIEL. I know her.

PEPPY (*sternly*). No, Daniel, no. You don't know her, Daniel. There was no fur on her coat. I walked into town and I walked home again, this is the story. I don't know what is happening with the buses today!

She laughs weakly, shaking her head.

DANIEL waits a moment and then puts his headphones on again and presses play on the tape recorder.

All that way! And do you know what I'm thinking, I don't think you do, I'm thinking wouldn't it be nice if someone cooked *me* some supper today, Daniel. But you can't, that's okay! It's okay!

PEPPY moves some things to make a space to put the pan down.

She rummages about and finds a carrot and a potato, they are quite muddy. She holds them for a moment.

The sound of arguing flares up aggressively through the wall from next door.

A woman is crying, saying, 'It's too late, there's no going back, you can't unsay things.'

A man's voice is shouting, 'Listen! Listen to me!'

A woman's voice screams, 'Leave me alone!'

A door slams.

PEPPY *doesn't react. She turns on the tap, water trickles.*

What shall I make for the supper, Daniel?

PEPPY *looks and sees that* DANIEL *has his headphones on.*

He can't hear me, he has his headphones on his ears, take the headphones off please, Daniel, I am speaking.

PEPPY *goes to him and gently removes the headphones again.* DANIEL *presses stop on the tape player.*

What shall I make for the supper, Daniel? Are you hungry? What would you like to eat?

DANIEL. I don't know.

PEPPY. And I don't know! (*Laughs.*) I don't know, Daniel! (*Suddenly looking around on the floor.*) Where's Charlie Brown? Where is he, Daniel? (*Calls.*) Charlie Brown!

DANIEL. What did the lady with the fur on her coat say?

PEPPY. Have you seen Charlie Brown, Daniel, has he been waiting here for me to come back with his biscuits because I didn't tell you this, Daniel, because I had only just finished telling you about the walk to town and the walk home again, and I forgot to tell you the really very strange thing, Daniel –

DANIEL. What colour is the dog?

PEPPY. So much to tell you that I forgot to say that the shops were not open, Daniel, can you believe it? It's true!

DANIEL. I know the lady with the black dog and the fur on her coat.

PEPPY. There was no fur, Daniel, you must remember to listen, I am telling you the middle part of the story, the important part! Nobody had opened the shops today! And Charlie Brown is waiting for his biscuits! The shops were not open today, what do you think of this most important part of the story?

DANIEL *doesn't know what to think.*

What do you say? You see!

DANIEL *doesn't know what to say. He goes to put his headphones on again,* PEPPY *gently stops his hand.*

I think I know what this is, Daniel.

PEPPY *starts to rifle through papers on the table.*

Let me see now, I think I heard something on the BBC Radio 4. I remember now, three days ago when I was listening to the radio before the batteries finished, Daniel, I wrote it down, the date I think, you will laugh when I show you!

DANIEL. The batteries ran out in the radio four days ago.

PEPPY. Yes! Oh dear! Where is this piece of paper?

DANIEL. The light came on to warn us seven days ago.

PEPPY. I am too busy to look at the light, let me see. (*Laughing.*) Something really very funny, Daniel, I think today.

DANIEL. You have to keep an eye out for the light because it tells you when the batteries are running low and therefore about to run out.

PEPPY. I can't find it now!

DANIEL. That's why there's a light.

PEPPY. What was it? They said the date and I wrote it down, yes that's it, I was in the garden and you were, I don't know where you were, I was in the garden and I was listening to the BBC Radio 4 and yes! They said about Jacopo Tintoretto, Daniel, because of course Titian was very jealous of Tintoretto, he was very jealous of him.

DANIEL. He was his student.

PEPPY. Really very jealous, Daniel, because – (*Angry.*) he couldn't teach him anything. He couldn't teach Jacopo Tintoretto because he had already taught himself! He was the most famous painter in the city, he was the most famous man in Venice, of course when he worked on the paintings for the Scuola di San Rocco.

DANIEL. And the Portrait of Vincenzo Morosini.

PEPPY. No, Daniel, this programme was about the Scuola di San Rocco, this was on BBC Radio 4. About the brushwork, of course the brushwork, we know all about it, but Titian was really very jealous of Tintoretto, yes, it was very sad really.

Pause. PEPPY *forgets to look for the piece of paper*

Of course *The Miracle of the Slave* made Tintoretto's style, the signature of the Venetian school in the late-sixteenth century, everyone said, he has been so influenced by Titian, yes, Titian, Titian, Titian! Tintoretto had his own, he was his own, yes, really so very different from the density, the impasto that Titian, it is different altogether, the way the light reflects, but really Tintoretto knew, he knew in his heart, he yearned for knowledge that no man could teach another. This is why Titian was jealous of Jacopo Tintoretto, Daniel, he had a greater skill.

A greater skill. Yes.

DANIEL. Gaugin didn't sell any paintings.

PEPPY (*irritable*). No, Daniel, this was about the Scuola di San Rocco in Venice, why don't you listen when I tell you things, it was on the BBC Radio 4! I listened to it in the garden. It really was a very interesting programme. St Mary of Egypt and the Mary Magdalen, the Scuola di San Rocco lifted the soul, no, it was very good, a very interesting programme about Jacopo Tintoretto.

I can't find the paper.

Daniel. Put on your listening ears, remember.

(*Sings at* DANIEL.) Good King Wenceslas looked out, On the feast of Stephen, Daniel.

When the snow lay round about
Deep and crisp and even.

Pause. She looks at DANIEL *expectantly.*

DANIEL *doesn't say anything.*

(*Sings at* DANIEL.) Brightly shone the moon that night,
Though the frost was cruel

DANIEL *doesn't say anything.*

Do you know, Daniel? Do you know?

DANIEL. What?

PEPPY (*sings*). Gath'ring winter fuel!

I waited for the bus for half an hour, no bus, no shops. What
do you think?

DANIEL *looks worried. He makes a move to put his
headphones on.*

Today is December the 25th, Daniel, it's Christmas Day.

DANIEL. Is today Christmas Day?

PEPPY. Yes. I think so. Why didn't Uncle Mannie ring us to tell
us, did Uncle Mannie ring us, Daniel? Where's the telephone?

DANIEL. Did the lady with the fur on her coat say it was
Christmas Day?

PEPPY. No, Daniel, she did not. Did the telephone ring today?
We have a big problem with the tap, what can we do, no
water on Christmas Day!

PEPPY *goes over to the sink. She turns on the tap. She finds
a bowl and starts to collect the slow trickle of water. She
stands there for a while collecting the water.*

As she stands there she sings in a very operatic serious style.

'Hither Page and stand by me,
If thou know'st it, telling.
Yonder peasant who is he?
Where and what his dwelling?

Sire he lives a good league hence,
Underneath the mountain.
Right against the forest fence,
By St Agnes fountain.'

PEPPY *has collected a small amount of water in the bowl.*
She turns off the tap. She looks around for the best place to
put the bowl of water.

Here let's put. Oh.

PEPPY *balances the bowl of water on something.*

DANIEL. The phone didn't ring.

PEPPY. No, no, Uncle Mannie rings on Christmas Eve, Daniel.
And he arrives on Christmas Day. Where is the phone please,
Daniel?

DANIEL. I don't know.

PEPPY. We have to phone Uncle Mannie, I think he has
forgotten us!

PEPPY *finds the phone.*

What is it, tell me the numbers please, Daniel.

DANIEL. 01904 –

PEPPY. Wait! Now then, let's see. 0.

She presses 0. Listens. Is satisfied that that's gone well.

What's the next number please?

DANIEL. 1904614322.

PEPPY. Wait! Daniel, stop this. You know I can't do it fast like
this. Now. 1.

She presses the 1 and listens again. Worried.

I don't think this is right.

DANIEL. Is Uncle Mannie coming for Christmas Day?

Pause. PEPPY *puts down the phone.*

PEPPY. Yes. I think he is.

She goes over to the kitchen.

He is on his way, he will be here any moment. Oh, We should have egg-lemon chicken and rice soup! We should have *yiaprakia*! Can you remember it? Oh what has happened to us? So many tears I could cry, for Mama and Baba and, we should have walnut spice cake, with sugar syrup, I was going to make it, can you believe it, Daniel, can you believe Christmas has come so all of a sudden? I'm not ready! I was going to make walnut spice cake and now it is here and. Can you believe I walked all the way in the empty streets! What a silly goat, look at that silly goat they said, they must have done, Daniel, with her empty shopping trolley and her, her. (*Laughs and shakes her head.*)

PEPPY *stands still for a moment staring at* DANIEL.

When she looks away, DANIEL *gets his notebook out of his pocket and makes a note in very small writing. Then he puts his headphones on and presses play.*

PEPPY *picks up a plate and spoon and bangs them together.*

Charlie Brown! Charlie Brown! Why am I calling him, there's no biscuits for him, he's given up waiting for me to come home, he's gone to catch a mouse I think, Daniel. Oh! I'm tired. When I tell Uncle Mannie I waited for the bus for half an hour and walked to town and home again! On Christmas Day! What will he say? 'You're falling apart, Peppy!'

She laughs and shakes her head.

PEPPY *stands for a moment and then has a burst of activity looking in drawers.*

Where's the Christmas tablecloth, I know we have it, Daniel, you know, the red flowers, the buds with the frost.

She sees DANIEL *is wearing headphones.*

He can't hear me. He doesn't know about the tablecloth, he doesn't know anything about it!

She starts to sing, the second verse of 'Good King Wenceslas'.

Bring me flesh, and bring me wine.
Bring me pine logs hither.

I don't know why they bring the pine logs to the forest! Why is this, who can explain this to me please?

She laughs.

Make room for the dancing!

Uncle Mannie likes to dance. Daniel! (*Shouts.*) Daniel! Take off the – (*Mimes taking off headphones.*)

DANIEL *takes off the headphones and presses stop.*

DANIEL. What?

PEPPY (*cross*). Help me! Help me to move the! We have to make it ready for dancing, it's Christmas. I must do everything on my own, why?

DANIEL *gets up really slowly and stands in the small space in front of his chair.* PEPPY *tries to get past him, she can't.*

Oh!

DANIEL. What?

PEPPY. Daniel! Lift up this chair please!

DANIEL *turns and starts to lift his chair but there is nowhere to go with it.*

No, this isn't right, Daniel, this is not how to do it.

DANIEL. What?

PEPPY. Mind, mind out the way please.

PEPPY *pushes past* DANIEL, *he loses his balance in the small amount of floor space and leans into some piles which slide to the floor. A tin falls to the floor with a loud clatter and money spills out.*

No! Look what's happened, this is not how things are done, this is not right!

DANIEL *is panicked, and spinning and not knowing where to be.*

He sits back in the chair and puts his headphones on.

PEPPY *is on her knees picking up the money and putting it back in the tin muttering.*

Now look, we have to collect all this up now.

PEPPY *collects all the money back in the tin, there is a lot, hundreds of pounds.*

When she stands up she sees DANIEL *has his headphones on and has not been helping.*

No, Daniel! Take it off, Daniel!

DANIEL *ignores her and presses play on the tape recorder.*

PEPPY *looks for somewhere safe to put the tin, she looks around and eventually finds a safe place high up out of the way.*

PEPPY *picks up a big dictionary and goes behind* DANIEL.

She hits him hard on the head with the dictionary. DANIEL *is shocked and takes off his headphones straight away and presses stop.*

PEPPY *puts the dictionary down and moves to the sink.*

Uncle Mannie will be here any moment!

DANIEL *silent.*

Can you believe that, Daniel?

DANIEL *silent.* PEPPY *turns the tap on, thin trickle. She turns it off.*

PEPPY *gives a little laugh.*

Daniel, do you remember when Charlie Brown sat on Uncle Mannie's hat?

DANIEL *silent.*

Yes, it was so funny when Charlie Brown sat on Uncle Mannie's hat.

DANIEL *silent.*

I remember it very well. I think it was yesterday!

DANIEL. It was December the 25th 2012.

PEPPY. Yes.

Pause.

Daniel. I think you knew today was Christmas Day.

DANIEL. When?

PEPPY. Today.

DANIEL *silent.*

It is not kind to let someone, someone who is loving and who does everything for you, it is not kind to let this person leave the house and walk all the way to town on Christmas Day.

DANIEL *silent.*

What do you think, Daniel?

DANIEL *silent.*

(*Sudden change of mood.*) Nevermind. I know you are sorry. And I am sorry too because I put the dictionary down on your head.

DANIEL *puts his hands on to his head.*

DANIEL. My head hurts.

PEPPY. I said sorry, oh dear, what a start to Christmas Day!

DANIEL. You hurt my head.

PEPPY. Yes. Well.

DANIEL. What dictionary is it?

PEPPY. I don't know. Daniel! 'What dictionary'! What a funny question. To ask.

DANIEL. I need to write it in my book.

PEPPY. No, Daniel, I don't think so.

DANIEL. I have to write it in my book.

PEPPY *looks at the dictionary.*

PEPPY. Oh look, Daniel, *The Canterbury! The Canterbury Dictionary of Hymnology*, here it is, I was looking here and everywhere for this one. What was it? On the BBC Radio 4, Daniel, they said something and I thought, now I will see what it says about this, and I looked but could not see it and now! Here it is! Let's wrap some paper on it, Daniel! Now where is the paper from the present Uncle Mannie brought last year, the blue paper, do you remember, with the stars. Where is this paper? Oh it feels like Christmas now, doesn't it, Daniel, and Uncle Mannie is coming any moment, and we have, we have the Christmas tablecloth!

DANIEL. That is the heaviest dictionary.

PEPPY. Oh no, Daniel, I don't think so.

DANIEL. It was the heaviest on my head.

PEPPY. Let's forget all about this now, Daniel, because it's Christmas Day.

DANIEL. I need to put it in my book about *The Canterbury Dictionary of Hymnology* on my head, Peppy.

PEPPY. No, I don't think so. We have too many things to get ready, we have to wrap the present before Uncle Mannie gets here, and – (*Looks about the room, anxiously.*) make a space for dancing.

PEPPY *picks up some papers and looks through them and then moves them to another place.*

Now. Mmmm.

PEPPY *moves some things off a box and opens the box. It's full of hangers and kitchen utensils and the lining of a waterproof coat.*

(*Pleased.*) Oh!

PEPPY *carefully and covertly wraps the dictionary in the lining of the coat and uses the cord from the hood to secure it like a ribbon.*

She gives it to DANIEL.

Happy Christmas, Daniel. And a Merry Christmas and
a Happy New Year!

Pause.

DANIEL. Thank you.

PEPPY. With best wishes from your ever-loving sister, Peppy.

DANIEL. Yes.

PEPPY. Open it!

DANIEL. Shall I open it now?

PEPPY. Yes, open it now, Daniel, open it and see what it can be.

DANIEL. Is it *The Canterbury Dictionary of Hymnology*?

PEPPY. Open it up! Let's see. It's Christmas morning!

DANIEL *opens it.*

What is it?

DANIEL. *The Canterbury Dictionary of Hymnology.*

PEPPY. Aah! Do you like it, Daniel, do you like your Christmas
present?

DANIEL. Yes.

Silence.

PEPPY. It's okay that you haven't got me a gift, Daniel, that's
alright, we are too busy. We can share this gift. What shall
we look up? I know this one – (*Sings very operatic.*) Good
King Wenceslas looked out! This is really for St Stephen's
Day, Daniel, we are a day too early. John Mason Neale, he
made up the words to this song, he went to my college in
Cambridge, did you know this, Daniel? Trinity College
Cambridge. No, I don't think so, look it up, Daniel, this
really is very good this present.

PEPPY *takes the book and starts to look through the
dictionary.*

Can you believe it? John Mason Neale studied at Trinity!
Before me of course, oh yes! (*Laughs.*) He was 1840. 1841 I
think, something like this, let me see. Neale Neale, where is it?

He was a priest, yes very nice this man, now look yes that's right! 'Tempus Adest Floridum', from *Piae Cantiones*! It's a spring hymn you see, Daniel, oh this is very interesting, this is a very good gift. (*Reads.*) Spring has unwrapped the flowers! Oh, Daniel! Can you imagine. Spring has unwrapped the flowers, da da da yes yes, celebrating the return of the flowers that winter had concealed and praising god for the joyful time of the year! *Gaudeamus igitur tempore incundo*! Oh this really is very interesting. Listen, Daniel.

PEPPY *sings with gusto to the tune of 'Good King Wenceslas'.*

Tempus adest floridum, surgent namque flores.
Vernales in omnibus, imitantur mores.
Hoc quod frigus laeserat, reparant caores,
Cernimus hoc fieri per multos labores.

PEPPY *finishes singing. Reads the dictionary. Very content.*

After a while DANIEL *gets his notebook out and starts to write.*

Are you writing about Mr John Mason Neale?

DANIEL. I am writing about you putting the dictionary down hard on my head.

PEPPY. No, Daniel, on Christmas Day you write about the gifts and the songs, not this other thing, no.

DANIEL. It's true.

PEPPY. No, Daniel, you have to practise listening, I don't think you are remembering about listening.

DANIEL. It has to be in the right order in my book, I can't miss bits out.

PEPPY *ignores him, she stands.*

PEPPY. When Uncle Mannie comes he will tell us stories about when he and Baba were boys, this is the right way to do things, that's how it should be, you see.

I wish I had made at least the walnut spice cake for Uncle Mannie, he would be so happy just to smell it cooking in the oven! Can you imagine what he would say? Oh! No point wishing, it's too late now, we have the dancing and the Christmas cloth, and oh, I miss them, Daniel.

PEPPY *cries.*

Too late, too late! I miss them all. Here round the table, all of us, and Mama standing here by the window when we come from school. Do you remember, Daniel? Of course, you remember it all.

What happens to us now? We're falling apart!

PEPPY *laughs weakly and lifts some piles of papers and moves them.*

DANIEL *writes in his book very small and close.*

Next door, a woman's voice can be heard calling, 'Come on! We're going. Now.'

She calls again. 'Ben! Come ON.'

Blackout.

In between the scenes we hear loud, furious and venomous, slightly distorted arguing between a man and woman. Smashing crockery. Crying.

Scene Two

Two weeks later.

Lights up suddenly on No. 23's kitchen/living room.

DANIEL *is sitting in his chair with a blindfold on. He is counting.*

DANIEL. Ninety-three, ninety-four, ninety-five, ninety-six, ninety-seven, ninety-eight, ninety-nine, a hundred.

He takes off the blindfold.

He looks around the room carefully. He stands up and looks around the room again.

He starts to move around the small amount of available space very slowly.

He knocks into a teetering pile of books.

He catches hold of one as it falls.

He opens it and reads.

He takes the book back to his chair and reads it.

BEN, *the boy from next door, is hiding in the room. He peeps out.*

He is eight, small for his age, an odd combination of confidence and geekiness. He is in uniform from a private school, his trousers are a tiny bit too short.

After a moment BEN *calls from his hiding place.*

BEN. Do you give up?

DANIEL. No.

DANIEL *carries on reading his book.*

BEN *eventually looks out. Stands up.*

BEN. You're not really playing this properly.

DANIEL *reads his book.* BEN *comes out and stands next to him.*

Why don't you hide and I'll count?

DANIEL *doesn't answer.*

It's quite difficult to play hide and seek in here because this room is really full. In my house it's better because there's more middle. Also more places to hide around the edges. The best place is the flat that my dad's renting temporarily in London Bridge, because all the cupboards are empty and you can get your whole body inside and shut the door.

DANIEL. Peppy has gone to Lewisham on the 484 bus and she'll be back at five o'clock.

DANIEL *looks at his watch. He continues reading.*

BEN. Can I test you?

DANIEL *hands* BEN *the book.* BEN *looks at the page.*

Okay. Say it from the – (*Counts in his head.*) seventh line down.

DANIEL (*closes his eyes and counts in his head*). More precisely, the picture is organised according to what might be termed a dialectical structure: the field is clearly divided into two parts that are deliberately contrasted in every detail but at the same time, by virtue of the overall pictorial conception, they are synthetically resolved into a full unity.

BEN. Correct. What is the last line on this page?

DANIEL. Titian further distinguishes levels of materiality, an upward scale from stone through jewelled cloth to unadorned flesh.

DANIEL *looks at his watch.*

BEN. When will you show me how to do it? Now?

DANIEL. Peppy is coming back from Lewisham at five o'clock.

BEN *puts the book down.*

BEN. I'm going to make one hundred pounds to cure cancer.

Do you think your mum will sponsor me?

DANIEL *looks worried.*

DANIEL. Who?

BEN. Your mum.

DANIEL. She died.

BEN. You said she'd gone to Lewisham.

DANIEL's confused.

Doesn't she like me?

DANIEL looks anxious.

It's okay, I'm used to it. Not many people like me, I think it's something to do with how I am.

DANIEL (*looks at his watch*). You should go before Peppy comes home.

BEN. No one at school likes me except a boy in the year below who hasn't got any hands because they got melted off in a fire.

DANIEL. Peppy will want you to be in your house when she gets home.

BEN. Why do you call your mum Peppy?

DANIEL. She's my sister.

BEN. Oh.

Pause.

I thought she was your mum.

DANIEL. She's not.

Pause.

BEN. I'll hide one more time.

DANIEL. I want you to go home.

BEN. Shall I tell you two things that I bet you don't know. No, three things.

DANIEL looks worried. He looks at his watch.

Henry the Eighth had a servant whose only job was to wipe his bottom and that is definitely true, okay? And the other thing is. Well, you know there are two 'c's in the word

Icelandic? Right, well there is no letter 'c' in the Icelandic language. Okay. And. Thirdly. If you folded a piece of paper fifty-one times, which you can't by the way, it would be thicker than how far it is between here and the sun.

DANIEL *looks suspicious.*

Try it, it's true. You will not be able to fold it that many times, definitely. Because that's how thick it would be if you did.

BEN *does a strange triumphant dance and then falls still and silent.*

DANIEL *puts his headphones on and presses play on his tape recorder.*

BEN*'s phone receives a text. He takes it from his pocket and reads the text and then puts the phone back in his pocket.*

Hey! Shall we read your diary?

DANIEL *doesn't answer him.*

After a moment or two BEN *moves around the room looking for a hiding place again. He finds one under a table behind some boxes. He curls up and hides.*

Some time passes.

PEPPY *enters in her coat and hat and carrying several big bags, one a large tartan laundry bag, others various plastic bags, a bag for life.*

Not shopping, just baggage.

She has been seriously rained on. No umbrella.

She waves at DANIEL, *he doesn't notice her.*

PEPPY (*calls*). Charlie Brown! Charlie Brown!

See what I've got you! Where is he now?

PEPPY *hits a spoon on a plate and starts to unwrap some fish from a soggy paper bag.*

BEN *comes out of his hiding place.*

PEPPY *sees him and it throws her. She looks away pretending not to have seen him, and then looks at him as if she has only just noticed him and looks surprised.*

Oh! It's you!

She does a small, casual laugh and a wave.

BEN. Hello.

PEPPY *bangs the plate. Pause. She bangs the plate again loudly.*

DANIEL *looks up.*

Can you sponsor me because I'm doing a sponsored walk?

PEPPY (*calls*). Charlie Brown! He doesn't like outside people inside, he doesn't know who is here! (*Laughs.*) He is thinking, 'Who is this? Why has this one come inside?'

BEN *hands her his sponsorship form.*

BEN. I am going to walk around Blackheath until I've walked ten kilometres.

PEPPY *is looking at the form, nodding.*

PEPPY. Yes, yes, yes, yes.

BEN. Nearly everyone on the street has sponsored me.

PEPPY. Yes that's good. Thank you very much.

Pause.

BEN. Are you going to sponsor me?

PEPPY. It's good yes.

BEN. You don't have to give me a lot. If you haven't got any money that's okay. Just like fifty pence or one pound is okay. And you don't have to give it to me now, because the walk is on Sunday.

PEPPY. Yes it's good, thank you.

Pause.

BEN. So.

Pause.

Yeah.

DANIEL *takes his headphones off.*

PEPPY. We wasted all that time this morning, Daniel. I have been rushing everywhere today to get the jobs done. I told you, you can't just, you have to have the proper equipment, for the, for the, for the class, Daniel, because you can't take part if you don't have your own brushes, you have to have your own brushes, I told you, people have to bring their own brushes, that's how it works, that's how they do it, Daniel.

DANIEL. I know.

PEPPY. People coming from this place and another place to the art class with no brushes, that's not how it works, you have to understand how they do it, I told you before but you don't listen to me. All that way on the bus, Daniel, without the proper equipment, no, no, no that's not how to do it, you see.

Pause. DANIEL *looks at* BEN, *embarrassed.*

BEN. So if you want to sponsor me you need to write your name on the form.

PEPPY. Oh yes, I see, good.

PEPPY *takes the form and writes her name very carefully and hands it back to* BEN.

BEN *looks at the form.*

BEN. Are you going to decide how much you want to sponsor me after I've done it? I suppose that's okay. Because you know No. 27, you know Mel and Nick?

PEPPY. Yes! All the, people.

BEN. Right well they put, like, an overall amount of ten pounds. Even if I only take two steps. But I'll do more than that obviously.

PEPPY. I see, yes!

PEPPY *is doing little laughs. And nodding.*

BEN. So you could do something like that if you want.

PEPPY. So many things to do. So busy.

BEN. Because it's for a cure for cancer.

Pause.

My dad told me not to ask you. I think it's something to do with because you are recluses.

Pause.

My dad's moved into a flat anyway so he won't find out that I asked you.

My mum's at work. She couldn't get a babysitter.

So. Yeah.

PEPPY *does a little laugh.*

From now on she ignores BEN *and just talks to* DANIEL

PEPPY. I have so many jobs to do I will be up all night getting ready to go to fetch Uncle Mannie. What are you doing, Daniel?

DANIEL. I am thinking.

PEPPY. Well this is no help to me.

I need a going-away bag, Daniel, where is this? (*Laughs.*) I don't know where everything gets to! I won't be able to carry, how can I carry all, all of the, belongings, without a bag?

DANIEL. I'm going to paint that tree tomorrow.

PEPPY. Of course, because Tintoretto pressed *feeling* into paint. His brushstroke, his mastery of light, this was a dance of the human and the, and the *spirit*. He was a visionary you see. And this comforted the people. Because of course the Church had no ears for this kind of thing.

DANIEL. Where are my brushes?

PEPPY. Oh, now he asks for his brushes! Now he says, 'Where are my brushes?!'

PEPPY *is looking through heaps of things for a bag.*

BEN. Bye then!

PEPPY. Oh yes, goodbye, thank you for bringing, this paper to show us, it's very nice. The next-door child is going now, Daniel, goodbye! Goodbye now!

DANIEL *puts his headphones on.*

BEN *loiters.*

BEN. There's a picture of one of those old tape players in my encyclopedia. Do you want to see it?

DANIEL *looks at* PEPPY, *unsure what to say.*

Next door the sound of SOPHIE *on the phone, she is raising her voice, we hear: 'Then you can fuck right off,' and 'You have no idea what I'm capable of, just you wait, you are going to get the biggest fucking wake-up call of your life,' and 'You self-centred dickhead, fuck you.'*

Pause.

Bye then.

BEN *leaves.*

As soon as he is gone:

PEPPY. Everything to get ready and the next-door child he is making us listen while he is telling us all about walking.

Are you hungry?

DANIEL. Yes.

PEPPY. You can have some of Charlie Brown's fish, I will cook it in a minute.

DANIEL. Where do you think the next-door child lives?

PEPPY. Next door, Daniel! Next door! You've seen him forever jumping up and down in the garden. Think before you speak please. You will make me mad with your nonsense questions. But I know you can't help it so I am not cross.

DANIEL *gets his notebook out and writes very small in it.*

PEPPY *empties things out of bags to find an appropriate bag to repack.*

DANIEL. I don't think he can live next door because he said he was going to sell his house for one-point-six-million pounds.

PEPPY. He lives next door, Daniel, please. I know this. He is telling lies all the time because he is a child.

Don't let him in if he comes around here again, Daniel, please.

DANIEL. Why?

PEPPY *doesn't answer.*

Why?

Pause.

I think he's going to come back after the walk.

PEPPY. Yes and we don't want to know about it. Don't let him come inside. We will say we are too busy and that he has to come back another time and he will forget and that will be that.

DANIEL. What if we're not too busy?

PEPPY. We will be very busy because Uncle Mannie will be here and we will be looking after him. We will have no time to write our name on pieces of paper every time somebody wants to tell us about their walking. This is true.

DANIEL. What if he doesn't forget?

PEPPY. He will. He is a child, children forget everything.

Pause.

I am going to say one very small lie to Uncle Mannie, it is really very small and I don't even know really why I am going to mention it to you.

DANIEL. Is it about Charlie Brown?

PEPPY. No.

DANIEL *opens his book and gets ready to write.*

No, Daniel.

DANIEL *is silent. He tries to stop himself opening his book but he is desperate to.*

I am going to tell Uncle Mannie that I made the walnut spice cake for Christmas Day and that you have eaten all of it.

DANIEL. I didn't eat all of it.

PEPPY. No, Daniel, listening, listening ears please. This is the small lie I told you about, this is it, I made the walnut spice cake and you have eaten it.

DANIEL. That's two lies.

PEPPY. I am going to say this to Uncle Mannie.

DANIEL. Why?

PEPPY. Because he will be happy that I made a walnut spice cake for Christmas, and he will be happy that you have eaten it. So yes, it is the right thing to do and I do not feel guilty about the lie.

DANIEL. Two lies.

PEPPY *carries on emptying bags and reorganising the contents into different bags.*

DANIEL *writes in his book furtively.*

PEPPY. This is what happens when people fall away, Daniel. You see? It is left so that one person has to go up and down to York collecting people and bringing them back. I don't want to leave you by yourself.

DANIEL. I like being by myself.

PEPPY. No. I don't think so.

Can you remember? I am twelve and you are ten and Mama has to collect a parcel from some people who had brought it back on the aeroplane? / And she is gone so long and we have to stay all alone and –

DANIEL. I was eleven and you were thirteen –

PEPPY. Yes, something, and we hear a noise in the back bedroom, we are so afraid! Ha! Is it a man with a knife? We don't know! We stay awake all night, I am holding a big heavy pan, and you are so afraid! 'Don't leave me, Peppy,

promise me!' This is what you say! You hold on to me like
this, haha! You never spoke this way, it was new! I remember
I am thinking, he never says he needs you, Peppy, and now he
says it so it means he is truly afraid. And when I know you are
afraid I feel brave, Daniel. This one time. Brave in my head
and brave in my blood all through my veins, yes, this is brave!
A door is opening inside me and courage is rushing in. 'I will
protect you, my brother.' Have I ever left you?

DANIEL. No.

PEPPY. No. That's it, you see.

DANIEL. Is my fish ready?

PEPPY. No. I am looking for a bag.

DANIEL. I'm hungry.

PEPPY. I will cook some fish for you when I have found the
right bag. I have to find the bag first.

Silence while PEPPY *moves things, gathers things, puts
things down in a different place. No obvious logic. She
unzips a large, full holdall and looks inside.*

What is this? I don't know. (*Laughs.*)

DANIEL. Where will Uncle Mannie sleep?

PEPPY. In Mama and Father's room.

DANIEL. The door doesn't open.

PEPPY. I know, why not? Because the room is full of the past,
I can't get inside.

DANIEL. The ceiling fell on to the bed, remember.

PEPPY. There are too many boxes everywhere, the piano music
from Grandma and Mama's clothes from the wardrobes in
the back room. We will have to move this. When do I have
the time?

He will sleep in our room, the mattress is hard, he will like
that. I can reach behind and open the curtains, he can look
outside, he will like it.

DANIEL. Where will we sleep?

PEPPY. No more questions please.

DANIEL. Where, Peppy?

PEPPY. On the floor next to this chair.

> DANIEL *looks around, worried about where there is room for them to lie down.*

Some cushions, some blankets, yes it's very good here, it is best. Some books here for us to read, stop asking questions, I am too busy.

> *Pause. Then suddenly:*

Daniel, I have a feeling rising up inside in my chest, like a wave is coming, I am afraid it will drown us both.

(*Laughs.*) But I have this feeling a lot and always I am wrong so I will ignore this and it will go away.

(*Calls.*) Charlie Brown! I think he will bring a mouse to show us in a minute.

Tell me something, Daniel, something to calm the voices talking in my head, tell me, come on, what?

DANIEL. No. I don't want to.

PEPPY. Stop it, Daniel, you know what happens when the voices are loud. Read to me from your book, Daniel, read me all the words you have written about, it soothes me.

> DANIEL *puts his headphones on and presses play on the tape recorder.*

> PEPPY *tuts and continues her fruitless business.*

DANIEL (*too loudly over the music on his headphones*). I'm hungry.

> PEPPY *moves into the kitchen, muttering, anxious.*

> *Lights down.*

> *Low hum of next door's television.*

Scene Three

Dead of night, heavy rain.

Front room of No. 23.

DANIEL*'s headphones and tape recorder on the arm of the chair.*

There is a scuffling sound outside the back door, and then knocking. Tentative at first, getting more pressing.

DANIEL *enters from the hall. He stands in the dark room looking at the back door*

The back door opens and BEN *enters, in his pyjamas, soaking.*

BEN. Hello. Can I come round?

DANIEL. Peppy's gone to York on the coach, she's coming back tomorrow.

BEN. Shall I come in?

Beat.

DANIEL. Peppy's gone to York.

They don't say anything for a while.

BEN. I'll just come in.

He closes the door behind him.

They are silent.

BEN *moves further into the room.*

You probably should lock your back door at night. Normally.

DANIEL. Why were you in the garden?

BEN. I climbed out of my bedroom window and on to the utility-room roof then I climbed down the trellis and jumped into the tomato plants and then I climbed through the fence at the bottom where the foxes have flattened it. My dad says we're going to have to fix that because even though it's actually your responsibility he says he can't be bothered to get into it with you so we might as well just get on and do it ourselves.

DANIEL. Why did you go in our garden?

BEN. We can play hide and seek if you like.

DANIEL. Peppy's coming back tomorrow.

BEN. Do you want a cup of tea? I can make it.

>DANIEL *looks anxious*.

>Don't you believe me? I know how to. I make it for my mum every morning. I take it to her in bed.

>So do you want me to make it for you?

>*Beat.*

DANIEL. Yes.

>BEN *goes to fill the kettle. He can't find a kettle.*

BEN. Where's a kettle?

>DANIEL *looks blank.*

>BEN *finds a pan and holds it under the tap and turns it on, just a tiny trickle comes out. He waits for it to fill, it takes a long time.*

>In my house water comes out loads quicker than this.

DANIEL. Where's your house?

BEN. Next door. Don't you know that? You're the next-door neighbour.

>BEN *moves some things off the top of the cooker to reveal a gas ring. He lights a match and lights the ring. He puts the pan on the flame. He looks over to* DANIEL *to see if he's watching him.* DANIEL*'s writing in his notebook.*

>I haven't even brushed my teeth, no one told me to.

>My pyjama bottoms are soaking wet, what shall I do?

>DANIEL *doesn't answer.*

>What are you writing?

>DANIEL *moves so* BEN *can't see and carries on writing.*

>Is it your diary?

DANIEL. Yes.

BEN. Will you read it to me?

DANIEL. Go back to your house.

I'm busy.

BEN. No you're not.

Pause.

DANIEL. I am.

BEN *stands for a moment and then goes to check on the water in the pan.*

BEN. I thought you wanted me to make you a cup of tea.

DANIEL. This time is not convenient for me.

BEN *takes the pan off the heat and pours the water into a cup. He looks around for tea bags, too difficult. He takes the cup to DANIEL.*

BEN. I can do it better at my house. We've got a kettle and tea bags.

DANIEL *looks at it.*

Do you want some milk in it?

DANIEL. Yes.

BEN *looks around eagerly for the fridge. He opens it and takes out milk, hands the carton to DANIEL, who pours milk into the cup right up to the rim, too full.*

BEN. Whoa, that's full.

Pause. DANIEL holds his tea precariously.

Do you like it?

DANIEL. Yes.

Goodbye.

BEN. Please.

Can I at least wait till my pyjamas are dry.

BEN *takes off his pyjama bottoms, he stands there in his pants.*

They're soaking. Can I hang them up? I'll go when they're dry.

DANIEL. They won't dry until tomorrow.

BEN. They might.

DANIEL. It's too long to wait. Put them back on.

BEN. I can't. They're wet.

DANIEL. You're not allowed in here. Go away.

BEN. I can't go out without any trousers on, can I?

Pause.

DANIEL *writes in his book.*

BEN *stands for a moment watching him, then suddenly snatches the book from* DANIEL*'s hands and runs to the other side of the room with it.*

DANIEL *(stands up, panicked, spinning).* No! Don't!

BEN. Your writing is like a girl's!

(Reads from the book.) Work in the studio to improve your ob-ser-vational and watercolour skills.

My cousin has writing like this.

DANIEL *tries to get to* BEN *across the room, stepping over and around the piles and boxes.*

DANIEL. Give it to me. It's private.

BEN. What are all these numbers?

DANIEL. Mind your own business.

BEN *(reading).* The grey marks on the side of the green dustbin prove that the scraping noise at six fifteen in the morning is the green dustbin and not the brown dustbin against the wall. Pay your council tax.

DANIEL *(starts reciting from memory).* How much council tax you pay, Reductions, Appeals –

DANIEL/BEN. When someone dies, Who is liable, Council tax standards, If you don't pay your council tax, Changes in your circumstances. The Problem of Expression 1. Some Mistaken Notions. How does a feeling get into an object?

BEN *stops*.

DANIEL. Health in Lewisham, Libraries.

BEN *goes over to* DANIEL *and hands back the book*.

BEN. How do you *do* that?

DANIEL *sits back in the armchair*.

DANIEL. Are you going to put your pyjamas back on?

BEN. Sorry about running away with your diary.

It was only a joke.

BEN *squeezes in next to* DANIEL *on the armchair. He gently takes the book from* DANIEL.

Shall I test you some more?

DANIEL. After that will you go back to your house?

BEN. Yes.

DANIEL *starts to recite from memory,* BEN *reads along in the book*.

DANIEL. The wind blew Peppy down. The lady with a zebra scarf held her hand and pulled her up. She had mints in a tin. She asked me if I wanted a mint. Peppy said I didn't.

BEN. Did you want a mint?

DANIEL. Yes.

BEN. I thought so. Carry on.

DANIEL. The 484 due at sixteen forty-nine is six minutes late.

BEN *tentatively rests his head on* DANIEL*'s shoulder*.

Taking inspiration from the gallery's collection, this course will focus on how to create a portrait. Explore the painting techniques of Rembrandt and the dramatic lighting of Caravaggio with artist Stephanie Carter.

Loampit Vale, Vicar's Hill, Cliffview Road, Harefield Road, Breakspears Road, we are now approaching Frendsbury Road, this is the 484 to Denmark Hill.

BEN. I get that bus! On the way back from piano! 'This is the 484 to Denmark Hill', that's exactly what it says! This book is so good. Carry on.

DANIEL. In Duccio's hands the Greek manner has become unfrozen, as it were, the rigid angular draperies have given way to an undulating softness, and the bodies, faces, and hands are beginning to swell with a subtle three-dimensional life.

You should have thought about that before you fucked one of your students, you repulse me.

In the staffroom at the doctor's they have a microwave. If you have a microwave you can have macaroni cheese. Or other dishes with a cheese sauce like cauliflower cheese.

DANIEL *looks at* BEN, *he has his eyes closed.*

Domestic violence, hate crime, youth offending, antisocial behaviour, emergencies, Lewisham pledge to the victims of crime.

Chronic ill health prevented him from taking a parish.

Sackville College was a charitable residence for the poor.

Charlie Brown has caught two mice and a bluebottle.

Giotto's *The Deposition*, for instance, can be described as conveying an intense feeling of grief and anguish.

Please knock hard. The bell is broken.

DANIEL *stops.*

Silence.

BEN *opens his eyes.*

BEN. It's like a picture drawn with words. Everything's on it.

Who's your best friend? You're mine.

Pause.

If I tell you a secret do you promise you won't tell anyone?

DANIEL *doesn't say anything, but he is listening.*

When I was four I had a brother. He can see everything that I do, and hear everything that I think. He's watching us now! I'm going to live with him when I'm dead.

Carry on.

BEN*'s eyes close.*

DANIEL (*reciting from memory, he speaks softly*).
Let us now our voices raise, wake the day with gladness;
God himself to joy and praise turns our human sadness:
Peppy is getting the 21:00 coach to York.
Up and follow, Christian men! Press through toil and sorrow;
Spurn the night of fear, and then, O the glorious morrow!

BEN *is breathing heavily.* DANIEL *sits for a while. Then he starts to write quickly in his book.*

Lights fade.

Scene Four

Tuesday 7th January 6.30 a.m.

Very slowly lights up as day breaks. The living room of No. 23 is steeped in early light from outside.

BEN *is asleep in the armchair by himself. He has been covered by a cagoul.* DANIEL *is not there.*

Through the wall SOPHIE *is calling* BEN*'s name.*

BEN *comes to, it takes him a few moments to work out where he is.*

Suddenly he jumps up, goes to the hall, changes his mind, comes back into the room, goes to the back door, stops, moves back into the room.

Stands still.

We hear the low blah of the radio from next door.

DANIEL *walks through the doorway.*

BEN *moves to the back door and barricades it with a chair.*

DANIEL *and* BEN *stand in silence together in the room.*

Lights down.

Sound of a car pulling up, car doors opening and closing. Next door's doorbell. Low voices from next door, several people talking.

Scene Five

Tuesday 7th January late afternoon.

DANIEL *is sitting with his headphones on.* PEPPY *is in the kitchen with her coat on. She opens the fridge and lifts some foil off a plate and peers under it.*

She doesn't look at DANIEL.

PEPPY. Well, I think this was your lunch today and it is still on a plate so this is a big shame, nevermind. I don't know what you want to eat! You are very hungry I think, you are starving hungry I expect. Well, I will have to prepare something even though I have had a very busy day and a long journey, I think I am like Odysseus after the fall of Troy, very long journey, very slow.

DANIEL. When is Uncle Mannie going to come downstairs?

PEPPY. All the way home to Ithaca, ten years travelling, Daniel! I am making a joke. I am not like Odysseus really. Oh dear!

DANIEL. Is Uncle Mannie in our room?

PEPPY *bangs a spoon on a plate loudly.*

PEPPY (*calls*). Charlie Brown! Charlie Brown! Where is this cat, I don't think he knows that I am home. I don't think he knows what a long journey I have had travelling all the way to the North of England and back again. Also he is just a cat and doesn't care! I know this.

PEPPY *takes off her coat and puts it down.*

DANIEL *stands up.* PEPPY *glances quickly at* DANIEL.

Where are you going?

DANIEL *says nothing.*

There is no reason for you to go upstairs.

DANIEL. Where are we going to sleep?

PEPPY. Down here like I said. It is all decided. It really is very exhausting for me to have to decide everything and then say it one and two and three times to remind you again. Really.

Pause.

What's the matter? Why are you looking all around like a big dog that has eaten a small dog's food. This is what you look like, Daniel, really.

DANIEL. I'm not.

PEPPY. Well, this is a case of a matter of opinion and this is my opinion so you see it is true. I have to do everything, I must rinse out my socks and make some food for Charlie Brown to eat.

DANIEL. And Uncle Mannie.

PEPPY. Yes. And Uncle Mannie of course. I only did not say this because it is one of those things that can go without saying so I didn't say it. I am very exhausted from the journey back and forth and. This Megabus is a very uncomfortable way to travel. I don't like it I wish I had got the train really.

DANIEL. Did Uncle Mannie want to get the Megabus?

PEPPY. Of course. He said, 'We must get the Megabus, Peppy, it is very cheap, we must save money, save money all the time save money. Come on, Peppy, take my hand,' he said. 'Yes. Very good.'

Oh it is very sad when no one uses your name any more. 'Come along, Peppy!' Uncle Mannie says.

DANIEL. I use your name. Peppy.

PEPPY. Oh you do not count.

> PEPPY *takes off her socks. She goes to the sink and turns on the tap. Hardly anything comes out.* PEPPY *holds the socks under the tap for a while, they get dripped on.*

This tap is really very bad.

Pause.

The faint sound of next-door's doorbell ringing.

A walkie-talkie crackles with broken voices.

DANIEL. Uncle Mannie can fix the tap.

PEPPY. No I don't think so, Daniel. He is too tired.

DANIEL. Tomorrow.

PEPPY. No I don't think he will come downstairs tomorrow or the next day. Not for a long time.

DANIEL. Did Uncle Mannie forget about Christmas?

PEPPY. So many questions.

DANIEL. Did you tell him I ate the spice cake?

> *There is a noise from upstairs.*

PEPPY. Shhh.

> PEPPY *listens.*

What's that?

DANIEL. Uncle Mannie?

PEPPY. No. He is not making a noise like this. This is something moving about.

DANIEL. It is Uncle Mannie moving about.

PEPPY. No, Daniel, it is not Uncle Mannie. He is fast asleep. This is not the kind of noise he makes.

Silence. PEPPY *listens.* DANIEL *is shifty.*

What is this creaking dragging noise?

Pause.

DANIEL (*anxious*). Uncle Mannie?

Pause.

PEPPY *goes to the door and listens.*

Are you going to see if Uncle Mannie is moving about?

PEPPY. What have you done, Daniel, what is happening? Something. What happened, Daniel, while I was away? What did you do?

DANIEL. I didn't do anything.

PEPPY *stares at* DANIEL

PEPPY. No, Daniel, tell me what is it, something is bad, I am catching sight of it in the corners, something is hiding from me in my own house and you are looking like this guilty dog, tell me.

DANIEL *looks away.*

Why do I have to find everything out myself? You have no idea how terrible this journey was, Daniel, always in a small space, people talking talking, all by myself on this very long journey, and now this. You with this funny face.

DANIEL. Not all by yourself.

PEPPY. I mean all by myself with Uncle Mannie. (*Runs at him and kicks him on his ankle.*) You are stubborn like a lame donkey in the way of the gate, and this is not the way to be, no, this is not how to do it when someone comes home after going on a very long journey by themselves. Not by themselves. (*A sob catches in her throat.*) But doing all the work by themselves, this is what I mean.

PEPPY *moves into the hall and looks up the stairs. There are flashing blue lights coming through the glass in the front door.*

And what is this stupid lights flashing on the street? Coming through the door all the time? What is this?

She tuts and shakes her head.

I go away for only one very small time and everything is different. This is why you have to stay in one place because when you go away everything moves around and then you don't know what to do and this is not good. No.

There is a knock on the door.

DANIEL *panics.*

DANIEL. Don't open it, Peppy, please, don't let them in!

PEPPY. Who is it? What has happened? Tell me.

DANIEL. Nothing.

PEPPY. Show me your book please, Daniel.

DANIEL. Are you going to open the door?

PEPPY. Let me see your book.

DANIEL. No, Peppy.

Stillness for a moment as PEPPY *finds courage.*

Then PEPPY *opens the door. Uniformed* POLICE CONSTABLE AMANDA GORDON *is there.*

PC GORDON. Good evening, sorry to disturb you, nothing to worry about, I just need to step inside and have a quick word with you if that's okay?

PEPPY. Oh yes, yes, come inside, that's good. We are just here, nothing to worry about either, so yes.

PC GORDON comes inside, and into the living room. DANIEL moves to the door as if to escape but gets caught up with PEPPY and PC GORDON coming in and causes a bit of a jam. He stays by the door hovering. PC GORDON comes into the room, she is obviously quite taken aback by the state of the room.

PC GORDON. Oh. My!

You've got a lot of stuff!

PEPPY. Yes, I have no time to sort it out, I will make some starts on it tomorrow I think.

PC GORDON. Have you lived here a long time then?

PEPPY. Oh yes, all the time really.

PC GORDON. All your life?

PEPPY. Yes! Longer than that I think!

PC GORDON. Well, you must have seen some changes in this area I imagine, very different just in the short time I've been working here so –

PEPPY. Oh yes, lots of changing, yes.

PC GORDON. Okay, well as I said, nothing to worry about. This is just a routine call because your neighbours, Mr and Mrs Banks? Do you know them, No. 21?

PEPPY. Oh yes!

PC GORDON. Okay, well, you might have heard about it, their little boy left home very early this morning and we are just trying to verify his whereabouts at the moment as he doesn't seem to have been at school today and his parents haven't been able to make any contact with him. Do you know the boy who lives next door? He's called Ben. He's eight. I expect you've seen him coming and going, have you?

PEPPY. Oh yes coming and going. Yes.

PC GORDON. Okay well, I'm sure you can understand that this is a very worrying time for Mr and Mrs Banks, because it's out of character for Ben to leave the house by himself and so they are very worried. Understandably.

There is a gap for PEPPY *to say something but she doesn't.*

DANIEL *hovers in the doorway, holding his notebook to his chest.*

Okay. Well, this is just a routine visit really, as I said. Can I sit down?

PEPPY. Yes, sit down this is okay, yes.

PC GORDON *sits in* DANIEL'*s armchair and takes out a notebook.*

Pause. PEPPY *doesn't say anything.*

PC GORDON. Okay. That's fine. And your name is?

PEPPY. Penelope.

PC GORDON. Penelope…?

PEPPY. Penelope yes.

PC GORDON. No, sorry, I mean, your surname is?

PEPPY. Angelis.

PC GORDON. And this is your husband? Is it? / Mr Angelis.

PEPPY. No, no this is not my husband! He is my brother.

PC GORDON. Oh your brother, / I'm sorry.

PEPPY. Yes my brother yes. My brother, Mr Angelis.

PC GORDON *looks a bit nervously at* DANIEL.

I haven't got a husband! Husbands don't like me, I don't know why!

PEPPY *laughs and shakes her head.*

PC GORDON. Does your brother want to come in? And sit down.

She looks around for somewhere he might sit.

PEPPY. He likes to stand there.

PC GORDON. Okay.

Slight pause.

Well, just a few questions about when you last saw little Ben, if you saw him, anything you can remember really.

PEPPY. No, I don't think I can remember anything really.

PC GORDON. Okay, maybe you remember when the last time was that you saw him in the garden? Or on the street. Out the window perhaps. Anything you can remember.

PEPPY. No. I don't know really.

PC GORDON. Was it today? Yesterday?

PEPPY. Today no. Because I went to fetch Uncle Mannie.

   I came back today on the coach, it takes a very long time,
   I couldn't sleep but some people they sleep very easily, very
   deeply as well I think, from York all the way to Victoria
   coach station some people.

PC GORDON. Okay. I wonder if we could just focus on when
   you last saw Ben because his parents are a little bit worried
   because they haven't been able to contact him, you see, not
   since he left the house very early this morning, okay, and so
   we are speaking to everyone on this street, asking people,
   anyone who may have seen him really, or seen anything
   unusual.

PEPPY. Nothing unusual no. I don't think so, no.

PC GORDON. Okay. So what about yesterday, did you see him
   at all before you went can you remember?

PEPPY. Before, yes, I saw him, yes. I had so many things to
   prepare, the boy he was talking all about paying him money
   for some walking in Blackheath, making me write down my
   name, telling me everyone has to give him money for this
   walk about cancer.

PC GORDON. Oh right, okay, so he was asking you to sponsor
   him for the charity walk?

PEPPY. The charity walk, yes. Saying all the people on the
   street must write their names on this paper.

PC GORDON. The sponsorship form, okay. So, he came to the
   door asking you to sponsor him, and, did he say anything
   that was unusual, or different in any way?

PEPPY. No, not unusual or different in any way, no.

PC GORDON. Okay, I'm just trying to get a picture of the
   dealings that you had with him, that's fine.

PEPPY. All the time wasted going on the bus to the class
   without the brushes!

   Pause.

PC GORDON. Okay.

She writes something in her notebook. DANIEL *starts to move erratically in the doorway, he makes a small sound.*

PEPPY. It's all very usual yes, all usual.

PC GORDON. Okay. Good.

And you were away last night, were you, in York overnight?

PEPPY. Because Uncle Mannie was not answering the telephone yes.

PC GORDON. I see.

PC GORDON *looks at* DANIEL *and smiles.*

And what about you, Mr Angelis, have you seen anything of Ben over the last day or two while your sister was away?

Long pause.

DANIEL *looks at* PEPPY.

PEPPY. What happened is this, you see, because he comes in sometimes. Perhaps when he has no key and his mother is at work. He likes to see my brother, he asks him questions all the time, because of his eidos, his eidetic memory, Daniel remembers where the words lie on the page, so he thinks he is a magician. Daniel encourages him, this is the problem, this is how the problem started, but I tell Daniel, I say every day, 'Don't let the next-door child into the house, put the chain on please, Daniel!' If you open the door just a small crack he pushes inside, this is what happens. So now. Daniel never lets him in. No. No. This is all finished now. So Daniel has not seen the boy, no. Not at all.

DANIEL *shifts awkwardly in the doorway, he looks very anxious.*

PC GORDON. Okay. Let's just. So Ben comes into your house?

PEPPY. Not now, no, not any more. Sometimes he comes in but I said to Daniel, 'This is enough now, this boy is not coming in this house any more. That's it. No more. Finished.'

Pause. PC GORDON *takes a moment.*

PC GORDON. Okay. Well, thank you very much, Mrs Angelis.

PEPPY. Miss Angelis.

PC GORDON. Miss Angelis, sorry. I think I just need to go and check up on some things with my colleague now, but thank you very much for your time.

PEPPY. I don't know all these people! I don't speak to them. They say the hedge is hanging too far on to the pavement, a woman with a pushchair has complained to the council about this. I don't know! They wrote me a letter, it came through the letter box with no stamp, but I don't know who it is from. It said, this is the third letter we have written to you about this issue, but this was a lie, I never received any letters before this one. Do you think the hedge is too big? I don't know how to make it small! They made a party in the street and I think the hedge was too big for this party maybe but I don't know! I found their rubbish in our blue dustbin, this one is not for rubbish like this I think. This is not what you have to do, the council is very strict about it, they put stickers on the lid with pictures telling you they won't collect the rubbish if it is wrong. It was some chicken bones, and some paper plates. It was spilling out on to the path you see.

PC GORDON. Okay, I'm going to stop you there, and go and have a quick chat with my colleague and someone will be back to speak to you again. Okay?

PEPPY. I had to go to York because Uncle Mannie was not answering his telephone, this is a very serious situation, Daniel knows this, I was too busy to write my name on the letter.

PC GORDON. Okay, I understand. Someone will be back to see you both.

PC GORDON *starts to leave.*

There is a big crash from upstairs.

Oh goodness, what's that?

PEPPY (*straight in*). Uncle Mannie.

Yes, Uncle Mannie is here.

PC GORDON. Okay, so your uncle lives here too, does he?

PEPPY. He wasn't answering his telephone, I had to go and get him. Yes. I came all the way on the coach with him.

PC GORDON *moves to the door.*

PC GORDON. I just need to step outside.

PEPPY. Everything has turned inside out!

PC GORDON. Thank you for your cooperation. I can see myself out thanks, that's fine.

PC GORDON *exits through the front door.*

DANIEL *looks at* PEPPY *in panic.*

PEPPY. What have you done, Daniel? What has happened?

DANIEL. Nothing, I didn't do anything.

PEPPY. Who is upstairs in our house, Daniel, tell me.

DANIEL. Uncle Mannie.

PEPPY. No, Daniel. Why are you lying? It's the boy, isn't it? Why?

DANIEL. I'm not lying, you said it's Uncle Mannie.

Stand-off.

DANIEL *goes to the armchair, sits down and puts his headphones on.*

PEPPY. This is very serious, Daniel, the police will not like this, they will be very angry, Daniel. Look at this! He is not listening to me.

PEPPY *pulls off his headphones roughly.*

I told you, Daniel, do not let this boy into our house. Why don't you listen to me? Now look!

DANIEL. I didn't let him in.

PEPPY. The police were here, have you forgotten, this is very serious indeed. The next-door child is upstairs, he is in the *wrong house*, Daniel, this is very bad news and lots of trouble.

DANIEL. He's not. It's Uncle Mannie. You said.

PEPPY. No, Daniel.

DANIEL. Where is Uncle Mannie?

PEPPY. I don't know. Not upstairs in this house.

DANIEL. Is he lost?

PEPPY. I am afraid so, Daniel, yes I think this is a true fact.

> Put the chain on the front door, don't answer the door, this is
> what I said to you, it is easy to remember, why can you not
> do this one thing, one thing I ask you, and all the things I do
> for you!

DANIEL. He came in the back door, he was in the garden.

PEPPY. You are a liar, Daniel Angelis, You are very cruel
saying these lies to me, this boy has made you a liar like
him. God hears your lies remember. Our mother would look
down on you and weep for the way you treat me.

DANIEL. What's going to happen?

PEPPY. The police will be angry about these lies. I will have to
make it right, always I have to do it, Daniel, I really am very
sick and fed up of this.

> Tell him he has to go home, Daniel, say it to him.

> DANIEL *doesn't say anything*.

> Say it, Daniel. He is out of character. This is very serious.

> Some people have dialled 999 on the telephone and called
> the police.

> DANIEL *stands up and leaves the room, he goes upstairs*.

> PEPPY *moves a chair and climbs up and reaches the money
> tin she had put on the high shelf. She opens it and takes out
> a thick bunch of notes*.

> DANIEL *reappears, followed by* BEN.

> PEPPY *is scared of* BEN, *she doesn't look at him. The three
> of them stand there*.

> (*To* DANIEL.) Did you tell him to go home?

DANIEL. No.

PEPPY. Say it please.

DANIEL (*reluctant, quiet*). Go home.

BEN (*to* DANIEL). Please, can I stay here?

DANIEL *looks at* PEPPY *hopelessly.*

PEPPY. How much money does the next-door child want for the cancer? Tell him we will give it to him if he goes home and never comes back again.

DANIEL *looks at* BEN *anxiously.*

BEN. I'm not doing the walk now because I have to go to Reading with my dad because it's my dad's weekend and he needs to be in Reading and we can't come all the way back just for me to do my walk.

PEPPY *offers the handful of notes clumsily to* BEN.

PEPPY (*to* DANIEL). He can have this money if he never comes to our house any more. Tell him!

DANIEL (*to* BEN). Do you want the money?

BEN (*looking at* DANIEL, *shakes his head*). No.

DANIEL *looks at* PEPPY.

BEN *is trying not to cry.*

They stand in silence.

DANIEL *looks imploringly at* PEPPY, *she is hard-faced.*

After a while, BEN *moves to the back door.*

Thank you for having me.

He moves the chair away from the back door and exits.

PEPPY (*furious*). You see? Now do you know why you have to listen to me? We don't know him, he is not our family, he tells lies and makes judgements, he thinks you are a clown, yes, a FOOL. He will go home to Mr and Mrs Banks and say everything about our private business, they will laugh at you, Daniel, I know these things, he will tell everyone at his school, say oh yes, my neighbour, he is this and he is this, a numbskull, he is some kind of imbecile, he is a halfwit, he is a birdbrain.

DANIEL. Stop, Peppy. He won't say that.

PEPPY. You don't know all the different kinds of people. I do, Daniel.

I protect you from them. Who said No, when they wanted to send you away? I did, Daniel. I said No, No, No. Every time. He has to stay always with me because he understands things only the way I explain them to him. I know the thinking he does inside. I had to leave my university because of explaining things to you!

DANIEL. Can I have my lunch?

PEPPY. No. I have to think hard, about what to do.

Pause.

DANIEL. I'm hungry.

PEPPY (*sharply*). Shhhh. I am thinking.

DANIEL *puts his headphones on. He writes in his notebook.*

I got off the coach and walked to his house. It was very windy and my umbrella was upside out and very useless. I was thinking I am wet even to my legs but this does not matter because I will soon be in Uncle Mannie's house and I can use the big towel. But he didn't answer the door. I knocked hard and I called his name very enormous through the letter box. I went to the back of the house and climbed up to the bathroom window, but nothing happened, the curtains were closed. The house was hollow and there was old air and silence all the way through to the back. I sat on the step to wait for someone to come – I waited all night and no one came.

It was really very cold on the step.

What are you writing in your book?

No answer. PEPPY *sees that* DANIEL *has his headphones on. She mimes for him to take them off.*

What are you writing?

DANIEL. About the next-door child going home out the back door.

PEPPY. Don't write that.

DANIEL. It's true.

PEPPY. Stop. This is not a good thing to write, no one will like it.

DANIEL. Who will read it?

PEPPY. Someone might.

DANIEL. Who?

> PEPPY *is thinking*.

PEPPY. Write a different thing, write that the next-door child came to the front door and you said, 'No, you cannot come in', like I told you. Write that you did as I told you, Daniel, everyone will like that better.

DANIEL. I don't want them to read it.

PEPPY. Do as I say please.

DANIEL. He came to the back door, it was raining.

PEPPY. No, not that, write that he came to the front door and you did as I told you and put on the chain.

> Go on. Write it.

> 'No, you cannot come in.'

> DANIEL *looks very anxious*.

DANIEL. Where?

PEPPY. Give me the book.

DANIEL. No.

PEPPY. Give it to me, this is very serious, Daniel.

> *Sound of a car drawing up outside, there are flashing lights through the glass of the front door. Voices. The crackle of radios.*

> Read me what you've written.

DANIEL. No, I don't want to.

PEPPY. Remember 999 and the police sitting in your chair.

> DANIEL *relents*.

DANIEL. The next-door child came in the back door. He made a cup of tea with milk. His pyjama trousers were wet. He took them off. He sat next to me. He read my book and tested me. My book is like a big picture with everything on it. He said I am his best friend. His head went to sleep on my shoulder –

PEPPY. No, Daniel, you can't write that.

DANIEL. I've written it already. It's true.

PEPPY. Ridiculous! This is not how you do things, give me the book please.

PEPPY *tries to grab the book.*

DANIEL *protects it fiercely.*

PEPPY *picks up* DANIEL*'s pen and holds it out to him.*

Cross that out, Daniel, we have to write some other things, no one is going to like what you have written, they will be angry about it and make you go away to live somewhere else without me.

DANIEL *looks worried.*

DANIEL. I can't cross it out. It's true.

PEPPY (*very stern*). Cross it out.

DANIEL *takes the pen. He crosses out his writing.*

DANIEL *makes a sound as if he has been wounded.*

Stop this.

Now. Write what I say.

The next-door child came to the door and I put the chain on like my sister Peppy told me and I didn't let him in.

Hurry up please.

Write, 'I said. "No. You cannot come in".'

DANIEL *writes slowly.*

Good this is better. It feels like there is air blowing through a window now.

PEPPY *laughs and makes a big exaggerated sigh of relief.*

Put this, 'And then I went to bed and fell asleep all night. Goodnight!'

PEPPY *laughs.*

DANIEL *stops writing. He looks at what he's written.*

Suddenly, an anger rears up inside him. He scribbles out what he has written. Then he rips out the page.

There is a knock at the front door. PEPPY *and* DANIEL *freeze.*

DANIEL. Who's that?

PEPPY. The lady policeman. She wants to come back in. Be quiet, Daniel, she will go away.

DANIEL (*whisper*). Why did you make me cross yesterday out of my book, Peppy? It's ruined it. / Put it back.

PEPPY (*whisper*). Shh, Daniel, we will forget all about yesterday.

DANIEL. He likes me.

PEPPY. Stop it, Daniel.

DANIEL. He does. I want him to come here. And I want yesterday un-crossed-out in my book.

PEPPY. No, Daniel.

DANIEL *starts to wail, he bends his book and rips more pages out, he throws the book, he gets up and flails around like a bear, he crashes into things and kicks and tantrums.*

PEPPY *watches coldly as* DANIEL *is wailing and spinning.*

After a while:

Stop it, you will wake Uncle Mannie.

DANIEL *stops. He is still.*

DANIEL. Uncle Mannie isn't here. You said it wasn't true.

PEPPY. This a different kind of true, like the front door and the chain.

DANIEL. Is Uncle Mannie here?

PEPPY. Yes. And tomorrow I am going to make lemon chicken and he will come downstairs and eat with us.

Look at your book, what a mess.

PEPPY *picks up the mangled book.*

It's all right, I will stick it for you tomorrow.

Pause.

The back door bursts open and two uniformed officers enter.

POLICE SERGEANT STEVEN HIBBERT *and* POLICE CONSTABLE AMANDA GORDON *move into the room.* SERGEANT HIBBERT *goes straight to* DANIEL.

HIBBERT. Daniel Angelis?

PEPPY. I am Penelope Angelis, I am the big sister.

HIBBERT. I am Police Sergeant Steven Hibbert, okay. Your neighbour's son, Benjamin Banks, has spoken to my colleague saying he has spent the night in your house, and obviously we need to ask you some questions about that –

PEPPY. He's lying, Daniel didn't open the door.

HIBBERT. And so, I'm arresting you now on suspicion of abduction of a child under thirteen –

PEPPY. No, no, he put the chain on, he did as I told him, / look here in this book.

PC GORDON *moves towards* PEPPY *and quietens her.*

HIBBERT. Your arrest is necessary in order to protect a vulnerable person, and to ensure a prompt and effective investigation.

PEPPY. Speak to me, he doesn't understand.

HIBBERT. I have to caution you that you do not have to say anything, but it may harm your defence if you do not mention, when questioned, something which you later rely on in court. Anything you do say may be used in evidence.

He looks at his watch.

The time is eighteen fifty-five. Okay. Do you understand what I've just said to you?

PEPPY. No, Daniel is not like those people, he won't understand you, / he can't.

HIBBERT. Mr Angelis, do you understand what I have just said to you?

(*To* PEPPY.) Is he a bit…?

PEPPY. No, no. / Excuse me please, sir.

HIBBERT (*to* DANIEL, *slowly.*) You're under arrest. Alright? Do you understand?

(*To* GORDON.) Have they got a car outside?

PC GORDON. He's going with you, isn't he?

HIBBERT. You might want to put a call into Social Services, looks like he's going to need a support worker.

PEPPY. I have to come with him, he won't manage on his own.

PC GORDON. He'll get each step of the process explained to him, we'll look after him, there's nothing for you to worry about.

PEPPY. He won't know what you are saying to him, / his mind isn't like that, he can't understand.

HIBBERT (*to* DANIEL). I'm just going to have to search you, Mr Angelis, alright? (*To* PEPPY.) Is he going to be alright with that, do you think?

PEPPY. Why? What for?

HIBBERT. I'm not putting the cuffs on you, mate, okay? But I'm going to have to do a quick search alright, just to check you don't have anything on you that you could use to harm yourself or someone else alright? So you continue to do as you're told and we're all good, but any mucking about and I'll have to put the handcuffs on you, is that clear yeah? He's a big lad, isn't he?

HIBBERT *searches* DANIEL*'s pockets. He pats him down.*

PEPPY. Daniel? Daniel, tell them you didn't do anything. Tell them the truth.

DANIEL *looks at* PEPPY*, desperate, lost.*

DANIEL. Which truth?

PEPPY. This is the problem! The police are here, Daniel, wake up. Why do you encourage him? Because you show off about your memory, isn't this true, Daniel? You like to be the important magician. I said to him Do. Not. Let. Him. Come in the house please. Now look!

DANIEL *looks very anxious, he is looking desperately to* PEPPY *for guidance.*

(*To* HIBBERT.) He was born with it, he used to sit in this room, here, and other times here, when he was five years old, I think maybe three, and he could draw the shoes of all the people at the bus stop. Even when the queue was very long and many people were there, all the shoes! Whether there is a lace or a buckle, all the ones. Please, he is not like the man you are talking about.

HIBBERT (*finishes the search*). Okay, good lad.

HIBBERT *starts to steer* DANIEL *towards the door into the hall.*

Off we go.

PEPPY. Please not yet!

As the front door is opened we hear the sound of a small crowd gathered, and a car engine, and police radios.

PC GORDON. They just need to ask him some questions, that's all.

PEPPY. He won't know the right answers to say. Ask me the questions.

PC GORDON. It doesn't work like that. He has to speak for himself I'm afraid.

PEPPY. Wait, he doesn't have his notebook, he can't…

PEPPY *comes running into the living room, she clambers over to the armchair. She is saying, 'Oh no, oh no, oh no' all the time.*

She grabs his headphones and the tape recorder and the mangled notebook and rushes back out into the hall.

(*Calling*.) Daniel! Daniel!

Sound of car doors closing, voices we can't catch.

(*Desperately calling*.) Daniel!

PC GORDON *is leaving. She stops in the hall.*

PC GORDON. Do you have somewhere else you can go, Miss Angelis?

PEPPY. Where?

PC GORDON. Some friends or family that could put you up for a few days?

PEPPY. No. I'm only, here.

PC GORDON. Oh, well somebody will come and talk to you about maybe going somewhere else for a few days because it's possible this house may have to be treated as a crime scene I'm afraid. Forensics will be in. They'll have to seal off…

PC GORDON *looks around at the boundary-less space.*

Send a photographer, take some bits and pieces away for analysis.

PEPPY. Which bits and pieces?

PC GORDON. It's usually bedding and clothing. You're better off out of the way to be honest. There are some missing pyjama bottoms, do you know anything about that?

PEPPY. No. I don't know anything about pyjamas because –

PC GORDON. Okay.

PEPPY. I went to fetch Uncle Mannie but when I got there the curtains were closed, I couldn't see inside. I sat on the step.

PC GORDON. Maybe start having a think about somewhere you could go for tonight.

PEPPY. Everybody's lost!

PC GORDON. Forensics will be here in the next fifteen minutes or so. I'll just wait for them here if that's okay.

PEPPY *goes back into the living room.*

Oh, and maybe stay out of the living room, Miss Angelis...

Slow build of sounds from outside and next door becoming louder.

PC GORDON *watches her for a moment and then makes a call on her radio to find out if forensics are on their way.*

PEPPY *goes to the sink. She finds a glass and turns on the tap to get water. It drips.*

She drinks the few drops in the glass.

Miss Angelis. I'm sorry, love, I'm going to have to ask you to come out of there please.

PC GORDON*'s radio crackles and brings the news of a stabbing in New Cross gate intrusively into the house.*

PEPPY *holds the glass against the kitchen wall and listens.*

The set begins to move and the bright, clean kitchen of No. 21 comes into view.

BEN *sits at the kitchen table opposite a uniformed officer and* SOPHIE *stands in the doorway.*

Lights fade on the room.

ACT TWO

Scene One

The same night.

The open-plan kitchen diner of No. 21.

Clean, sleek, white work surfaces.

BEN *is seated, opposite* NICHOLS, *a plain-clothes detective constable.*

SOPHIE *is standing in the kitchen, tearful, shaky.*

Another DC *sits at the opposite end of the table taking notes.*

NICHOLS. Mum's here. So if you want to stop, for any reason, you can just tell me, or tell Mum, okay? And all you need to do is answer my questions as honestly as you can and if there's anything you don't want to answer that's fine as well, you can just say, 'I don't want to answer that', or tell Mum, okay? Is that all right, Ben?

BEN. What sort of questions?

NICHOLS. Well, just about what happened last night and today, what took place, you can stop me if you don't understand or if, you feel uncomfortable –

BEN. What if I get one of the questions wrong?

NICHOLS. No, you can't get it wrong, it's not that kind of question, okay? It's not a question you can get wrong, / you just have to –

BEN. What kind of question is it?

SOPHIE. Ben, just answer the questions truthfully, you can't get them wrong.

NICHOLS. I tell you what, / I'll just get started, shall I?

BEN. I got eight out of ten in my French test at school because I spelt *la fenêtre* wrong, and something else.

NICHOLS. Yes well, / this isn't a test.

SOPHIE. Just start. It's not a test.

SOPHIE*'s phone rings*.

BEN. *Fenêtre* means window.

NICHOLS. Does it?

SOPHIE. Hang on, sorry I have to get this.

NICHOLS. Oh, okay.

SOPHIE. Hi hi. Yes he's fine, he's safe, he's fine.

Sorry, excuse me, one second.

SOPHIE *leaves the room*.

NICHOLS *smiles at* BEN.

NICHOLS. We'll just wait for Mum.

BEN. It's probably Dad.

NICHOLS. Yes.

BEN. He's got a girlfriend called Aoife, you spell it A–O–I–F–E. It's Irish. She doesn't speak in Irish and she doesn't live in Ireland. She lives in Reading. She was a secret girlfriend but now she's just a normal girlfriend.

NICHOLS. I see.

Are you good at French then?

BEN. I'm fourth best in my class. Emil is number one, but he actually *is* French so that doesn't really count. I'm better at maths than Emil. I'm probably joint second at maths in my class, but Ivor might be leaving to go to boarding school and then I'll be joint first. With Jack T.

SOPHIE *returns*.

SOPHIE. His father just wants to. Do you mind if he…?

SOPHIE *holds her mobile to* BEN*'s ear*.

BEN. Hello.

Yes.

Yes, I'm okay.

Okay.

SOPHIE (*to* NICHOLS). He wanted to hear his voice, I said you were in the middle of…

(*To* BEN.) Tell Dad you'll call him later, say bye.

BEN. I have to go.

SOPHIE *takes the phone from* BEN*'s ear.*

SOPHIE. He'll call you later, Simon, we're in the middle of a…

Yep.

Yep. Okay.

SOPHIE *hangs up.*

Sorry, I did say. He wouldn't listen.

NICHOLS. Alright, so before we start, do you have any questions, Ben? That you want to ask me?

BEN. Have you seen loads of dead bodies?

NICHOLS *laughs, looks at* SOPHIE.

SOPHIE. Just start. He's fine.

SOPHIE *hovers behind* BEN*, she is very restless and anxious.*

NICHOLS. Okay then, Ben, so as I said, I'm Detective Constable Nichols, okay, and I'm going to ask you a few questions. So, can you talk to me a little bit about how you came to be next door last night with Daniel Angelis?

BEN. Is that question number one?

NICHOLS. Yes.

BEN. I climbed out of my bedroom window and jumped on to the utility-room roof then I climbed down the trellis and then

I climbed through the fence, no hang on, first I jumped into the tomato plants, and then I squeezed through the fence at the bottom where the foxes have broken it.

NICHOLS. I see.

Why did you do that, Ben?

BEN. Because I can't reach the bolt on the back door, well, I can if I stand on a chair, but it is really stiff.

NICHOLS. Okay. But why did you decide to go into next door's garden? In the middle of the night. Did you notice what time it was?

BEN. It was really late. Later than midnight.

NICHOLS. Later than midnight, okay. But you didn't look at a clock, you don't know an exact time?

BEN. No.

NICHOLS. And why did you go into next door's garden at that time?

BEN. To go and see Daniel.

NICHOLS. That's quite late to go and see someone, isn't it?

BEN. Yes.

BEN *throws a look at* SOPHIE.

NICHOLS. That's all right. Don't worry.

Had Daniel asked you to come and see him?

BEN. No.

NICHOLS. Because if he had asked you, that's okay to tell us. Even if maybe he had asked you not to tell anyone, it's okay to tell us if that's the case.

BEN. He didn't ask me. I thought of it by myself.

NICHOLS. And what made you think of it, can you remember?

BEN. I was just wondering what he was doing.

NICHOLS. You're doing really well, Ben, you're answering these questions really well.

No one's going to be cross with you, if you tell us something that you think you shouldn't.

BEN. Like what?

NICHOLS. If someone told you to keep a secret.

BEN. About what?

NICHOLS. About anything. Has someone told you to keep a secret?

Pause.

BEN. No.

NICHOLS. Just tell us the truth, whatever the truth is, and you won't get into trouble.

BEN. Will Daniel get into trouble?

Pause.

NICHOLS. Tell me about Daniel, Ben.

BEN. Like what?

NICHOLS. Well, what do you and Daniel talk about?

BEN. Loads of things.

NICHOLS. So when you went to see him last night, to see what he was doing, what did you talk about then?

Pause.

BEN. I don't know.

NICHOLS. That's okay. It's difficult to remember things sometimes, isn't it?

BEN. Is Daniel going to get into trouble?

NICHOLS. Well.

SOPHIE (*a bit angrily*). You must remember what you talked about, come on, Ben. No one's going to be angry.

NICHOLS. Okay.

BEN. Why are you being angry then?

SOPHIE. For God's sake, Ben, just tell us what happened.

BEN. Nothing.

NICHOLS. Okay. Let's just.

SOPHIE. Obviously something happened, you were there all night and all day, / what were you *doing*?

BEN. You said you wouldn't be angry –

NICHOLS. Ben. The reason that Mum's getting upset, she's not angry, okay. Are you, Mum?

SOPHIE *has her head in her hands.*

The reason Mum's getting a bit upset is because she's been very worried.

BEN. Daniel's my friend.

SOPHIE. He is *not* your friend, Ben.

BEN. He is.

NICHOLS. Okay.

BEN. I don't want him to get into trouble.

NICHOLS. That's understandable. I can understand that.

BEN. Because I think I'm his only friend.

NICHOLS. Does he tell you that? Does he tell you you're his only friend?

BEN. No.

NICHOLS. But you think you might be.

BEN. Yes. Because he doesn't really go out that much. And he's not really that good at talking to people because he says weird stuff and if you don't know him you might think he was scary. But I know him so I'm not scared of him.

SOPHIE. Jesus Christ.

NICHOLS. That's fine, you are doing really well, Ben. You are being really helpful. Is it alright if I ask you some more questions about Daniel?

BEN. Like what?

NICHOLS. What sort of things do you do when you are at Daniel's house?

BEN. Loads of things.

NICHOLS. Like what?

BEN. Play hide and seek.

NICHOLS. Who hides, you or Daniel?

SOPHIE. Oh my God.

BEN. I hide. He's too big to hide because there's not much space in Daniel's house. Have you seen his house? He has so many things squashed in everywhere so there's no space for him to hide. I'm small and expert at hiding so I can always find somewhere good.

NICHOLS. So you hide and then he finds you, does he?

BEN. Actually, he's not very good at seeking. He forgets and just reads a book or sometimes listens to his music.

NICHOLS. Right.

BEN. He is so funny.

NICHOLS. Does he make you laugh?

BEN. Yes. He is the funniest person I have ever met. And the cleverest. He has lots of books and we look at them together and he can remember everything that's on the page when he's not looking at it. And I test him and he always gets it right and he's going to teach me how to do it. He has loads of books with pictures in and some of them are really funny.

NICHOLS. What kind of pictures are in the books?

BEN. Some ones with ladies with no clothes on and there's one with a baby with no clothes on and you can see his willy sticking out. Daniel says it's not meant to be funny, I think they're virgins. Daniel writes a secret diary all the time, and I'm the only person that's allowed to read it.

The front doorbell rings. The DC *leaves the kitchen.*

NICHOLS. Okay, good, so what kinds of things does he write in the diary?

BEN. Everything that happens to him.

NICHOLS. You're being very helpful, Ben. Are you okay? Are you feeling okay?

BEN. Yes.

NICHOLS. Good.

BEN. Is Daniel at his house now?

NICHOLS. You don't need to worry about that, Ben.

BEN. Is he?

NICHOLS. Shall we just answer a couple more questions and then…

BEN. I'm a tiny bit bored of answering questions.

NICHOLS. I know, you're doing really well, just a couple more and then we're done for now.

BEN. All right.

BEN *throws a look at* SOPHIE.

NICHOLS. So Daniel didn't ask you to come to his house last night, Ben, is that right?

BEN. You already asked me that question.

NICHOLS. I know, I'm just checking I've got that right. So you said you woke up and decided to go and see what Daniel was doing –

BEN. I didn't wake up, I was already awake.

NICHOLS. I see, so you were lying awake and you thought, I know, I'll go and see what Daniel's doing, is that right?

Pause.

BEN. Yes.

The DC *returns holding a large paper bag with a see-through window in. She gives it to* NICHOLS *and whispers in his ear.*

NICHOLS. Okay, and you were in your pyjamas, were you?

BEN. Yes.

Are those my pyjama trousers in that bag?

NICHOLS. Yes, I think so. Can you see through that window, do they look like your pyjamas?

BEN. Yes.

BEN *looks at* SOPHIE.

Am I in trouble now?

SOPHIE. Just keep answering the questions, Ben.

BEN. Why are you crying?

SOPHIE. I'm not crying, it's okay, answer the questions the policeman's asking you.

BEN. I only took them off because they were wet.

SOPHIE. Look at the police officer, don't keep turning round to look at me.

NICHOLS. Did Daniel tell you to take them off?

BEN. No, they got wet from the rain.

NICHOLS. And what happened after that?

BEN. When?

NICHOLS. After you took your pyjama bottoms off. What did you and Daniel do then?

Can you remember?

BEN. Yes.

I tested Daniel on his diary and then we went to sleep.

NICHOLS. Okay. You're doing really well, one last question and then you can have a break, did Daniel touch you anywhere on your body, Ben? While you were looking at his diary.

BEN. Yes.

NICHOLS. Can you show me where he touched you on your body.

BEN. Here.

BEN stands up and runs his hand down the whole right hand side of his body.

NICHOLS. Did he stroke you like that, down the side of your body?

BEN. No. Of course not. Why would he do that?

NICHOLS. Okay so how did he touch you on your body there?

BEN. Because I sat next to him in his chair and our bodies sort of squashed up together.

NICHOLS. I see. Do you want a little break, Ben? Do you want a drink of water?

BEN. Am I in trouble?

NICHOLS. You're not in trouble, not at all.

You're doing really well.

So how about a drink, Ben, Is that okay, Mum?

BEN. Can I have it in my Harry Potter mug?

SOPHIE. I don't know where it is, Ben, just have a glass.

BEN. Maybe in the dishwasher.

NICHOLS (*to* DC). Can we get hold of this diary please?

The DC nods and leaves the room.

BEN. You can't read his diary, it's secret.

NICHOLS. Don't worry about that –

BEN. Only me and him read it, you can't!

SOPHIE opens the dishwasher and finds the Harry Potter mug, she lifts it out and drops it and it smashes on the floor. Gasps.

SOPHIE. Aaaargh.

NICHOLS. Oh no!

SOPHIE (*furious*). My God, Ben, I must have told you a thousand times not to put mugs under that, lip bit, they catch and then flip out and now look, / well, it serves you right.

BEN. That was my special mug.

SOPHIE. I know it was, well, it's smashed now, so. Maybe now you'll listen to me / when I tell you things.

NICHOLS. That's a shame, / nevermind.

BEN. You smashed it.

SOPHIE. I smashed it?

BEN. It wasn't even me that put it in the dishwasher.

SOPHIE. Well, who did then? Who did? I don't use that mug, do I? God, look at this, it's gone everywhere, I'm going to have to pull everything out. Because I really need to be doing this right now.

BEN *stands up*.

Sit down –

BEN. I'm going to get the dustpan –

SOPHIE. You'll cut your foot, I'm not spending all night in A and E. Not after last night.

NICHOLS *watches*.

BEN. You said you wouldn't be angry with me –

SOPHIE. Just sit still, lift your feet up.

BEN. Why are you angry with me?

SOPHIE. I'm not, / I'm just clearing this mess up.

NICHOLS. I think everyone's just tired and upset after. Because Mum and Dad were very worried about you, weren't they –

SOPHIE. Well, Mum was.

SOPHIE *is sweeping the pieces of mug into a dustpan*.

BEN. I want to stop doing questions now. I haven't even had supper.

NICHOLS. I've just got a couple more questions, you're doing really well, Ben, I'll be as fast as I can.

BEN. It's going to be a really late night.

They sit in silence as SOPHIE *sweeps. She tips the pieces into the bin.*

That was my favourite mug in all the world and now it's got smashed and I'll never be able to drink out of it again.

Scene Two

Wednesday 8th January. Late morning.

The front room of No. 23. Everything has been piled up in one corner. The space looks entirely different and tampered with.

PEPPY *has two coats on. She looks as if she hasn't slept, she is ragged, ghostly.*

The front door is open.

GARETH *stands in* PEPPY's *living room.*

GARETH. My God.

This is. Wow.

GARETH *is looking round the room in amazement.*

PEPPY. My brother has never spent a night outside of this house before, not in our whole life.

GARETH. Really? I'd heard you had been here for years, but, wow.

PEPPY. Yes and only three times without me since 1988.

GARETH. Unbelievable.

PEPPY. This is the truth.

GARETH. So how long has this house been in your family?

PEPPY. 1959. My father bought this house with his brother.

GARETH. And how much did he pay for it, if you don't mind me asking?

PEPPY. Three thousand pounds, three thousand one hundred pounds something like this.

GARETH. My God.

PEPPY. Yes it was.

Pause.

I think it is worth more than this now.

GARETH (*laughing*). Yes, just a bit!

GARETH *looks at* PEPPY, *she's not laughing.*

(*Joking/testing water.*) Yeah, how about I give you ten grand for it!

GARETH *laughs.*

Pause.

PEPPY. When is Daniel coming home?

GARETH. Sorry?

PEPPY. This is a bad and serious situation and a really very big mistake.

I am very worried about my brother sleeping at Lewisham police station, he will be very afraid and will not understand why he is not at home with me.

GARETH. Right, yes.

Well. The police have to do their job, don't they. They get twenty-four hours, don't they, before they have to release or charge. Or is it forty-eight hours, I don't know, I used to watch *The Bill.*

Pause.

PEPPY. Who are you?

GARETH. Yeah sorry, I'm so knocked for six by the interior of the house, I've wanted to cop a look inside for ages, no, no, sorry, I was just going to say, you know, hi.

He holds out his hand for a very brief moment.

Umm, we haven't like had a chance to meet you or anything before now, and yeah, obviously it's a slightly awkward scenario, but the front door was open, so I thought I'd seize the day.

PEPPY. When is Daniel coming home?

GARETH. No! God, you've made me feel bad now! Barging my way in! No, I'm nothing to do with all this! What it is, it's just, well, to do you a favour really more than anything, my partner's sister, my sort of sister-in-law-type thing, her and her bloke, they've been holding out for a place around here for bloody ever, and as you probably know, maybe you don't actually, well, houses go pretty quick round here, half an hour No. 30 was on the market, snapped up! German businessman, wrote a cheque, bish bash, thank you very much, job done. So, I was just going to pop in and say, you know, *if*. You know, *if*, because obviously I have no idea what your plans are, but, you know, *if* you were looking to make a quick-getaway type of thing, you know, cut loose, make a clean break or whatever, obviously now that things have sort of come to a bit of a, you know, head, type of thing. Then.

Pause.

PEPPY. Are you the police?

GARETH. No! I'm just. My partner's sister is looking to buy a house.

PEPPY. Oh.

Pause.

You look like yesterday's policeman.

GARETH. No! I'm, umm, a web designer. My partner and I. We're No. 12.

PEPPY. Do you know when Daniel's allowed to come home?

GARETH. No. Of course not! I don't know anything other than what everyone's been saying.

PEPPY. No one's been saying anything. To me.

GARETH. Well. Just the basics, about the grooming, and the boy held here overnight. You'll know more about it than me. I don't know the details obviously. But I've got to be honest it's bloody shocking, on your own doorstep. I mean it must have been a shock for you too, under your own roof, but for us parents, especially, it really makes you think. So, I just thought, you know, whatever happens now, you might not want to hang around here after this. You know, so perhaps.

GARETH *looks around the room.*

So that's all the original cornicing, isn't it, and the fireplace. So is this what it was like back when your father bought it? It doesn't look like anyone's done anything to it for donkey's years.

PEPPY. I am busy. I am waiting for my brother to come home. I have to get everything ready.

Pause.

GARETH. Look. I don't know your brother obviously. I've only seen him out the window.

But. You know, most people think there's a reason they've got him in a police cell and it's.

Most people think. Something's not right.

And you know, maybe, I mean it's really quite likely, he might not be coming home, yeah? Do you know what I'm saying? No-smoke-without-fire type of thing.

Pause

PEPPY. Please go out, please.

GARETH. Sorry, I don't want to upset you, I'm just saying, you should maybe consider some options, and *if* you were thinking of moving on, which you know, could be a really good thing to do, in these circumstances, that's all I'm saying, it's good to be realistic, this isn't just going to go away. Well, my partner's sister, as I said, is looking to buy. In this area. And not being rude but, this is hardly an estate agent's dream! You know, how about we don't even need to involve them –

PEPPY. This is my own home and if you paid me fifty thousand, even a hundred thousand, I would never leave this house.

GARETH *is staring at her.*

GARETH. Look, if you'll just give me two minutes of your time. Listen, what's your name? Sorry I don't even know your name.

PEPPY *doesn't say anything.*

Okay, well, I'm Gareth okay, and my partner Lou. We live just over the road, grey door. Look. I don't think you fully appreciate how much property has gone up. I could, offer you the amounts you just said. (*Pause.*) I could, you know I could offer you double that. You know. Triple that.

PEPPY. My parents are here. In the walls and the floorboards and the bricks of this house. This is not only your street with only your stories.

GARETH. No, of course. It's just.

Pause.

This is a very family-orientated street, you know, what with it being in the catchment for St George's. These things hang in the air, leave a nasty taste. Word gets out. Feelings run high. I'll be blunt. I can't see how this is realistically going to work with you and your brother, you know. I don't know how happy you'd be here. After this.

PEPPY. We were born in this house.

GARETH. It's not you, no one's got a problem with you. It's just, you know, this business with your brother.

PEPPY *moves to the sink and starts to fill a pan of water under the tap.*

The water comes out in a thin trickle.

Look.

PEPPY *tuts.*

Let's wait and see the outcome of all this. It's early days.

PEPPY. Hurry up please, water.

GARETH. Our tap used to be slow like that. When we first moved in. We thought there was a problem with the water pressure in the tank, but actually it was just some debris lodged inside the faucet. It's quite easy to sort out, you just have to unscrew all the bits and give it a good rinse.

I can have a look if you like.

PEPPY *keeps her back to him.*

Okay well, another time. Maybe you'll have a think. I can come back. I tell you what.

He takes a card from his wallet in his pocket.

This is my card, okay, just ignore the. That's my email, okay. And mobile number. If you have any thoughts, need any advice even, about moving on, or.

Pause.

It would just be good to be able to get my wife's nephew on the list for the nursery at St George's. Then they'd be in the same class, the cousins. That's not your problem. Look, don't worry about it, it's okay.

GARETH *turns to leave.*

PEPPY. Why do you put letters in my door?

GARETH. When? I don't.

PEPPY. Yes. About the hedge.

GARETH. Oh, that's not us.

PEPPY. Who is it?

GARETH. I'm not sure really, I might have read something on the WhatsApp group about it, a couple of months back, I think it's just that maybe some people have had some trouble walking past without stepping off the pavement into the road. If you've got a buggy, and small children. It's quite overgrown.

PEPPY. Some people, oh.

Pause.

GARETH. Yeah.

Okay. Well. Sorry for.

GARETH *exits through the hall.*

Through the wall we hear next-door's doorbell.

PEPPY *stays very still for a moment, listening. Distant thud of their front door closing, low voices.*

PEPPY *starts banging on a pan with a spoon and calling for Charlie Brown.*

Scene Three

Kitchen of No. 21.

We can hear PEPPY *banging on a pan and calling for Charlie Brown through the wall.*

BEN *sits at the kitchen table, he is in his school uniform. He is drinking from his Harry Potter mug which has been superglued together.*

NICHOLS *sits opposite him.* SOPHIE *stands.*

SOPHIE. He wanted to go to school, I'm tempted to let him. He seems fine, and it's some kind of normal, I suppose. I said maybe he could go in after lunch. Would that be alright, do you think?

NICHOLS. Have the school been in touch? Since yesterday.

SOPHIE. Mrs Paige left a message but I haven't spoken to her.

BEN. Would I be school dinners?

NICHOLS. Let's see how you feel shall we.

BEN. I want to go.

SOPHIE. We know that, I've just said.

Pause.

NICHOLS. Okay, well, I don't know if you two have had a chance to talk any more since yesterday evening –

SOPHIE. Not really. Ben was tired, weren't you, Ben?

NICHOLS. I see you've stuck your Harry Potter mug back together, that's a good job.

SOPHIE. His dad was here, briefly. Always the hero.

BEN. Is Daniel still in prison?

SOPHIE. Not in prison, I said he was at the police station.

NICHOLS. He's just answering some questions that's all, just so we can make sure everyone's safe, okay?

BEN. Where did he sleep?

NICHOLS. He was perfectly comfortable, nothing to worry about.

I'm just going to ask you a couple more questions, Ben, is that okay?

BEN. No.

NICHOLS. It's not okay?

BEN. No.

SOPHIE. Ben, don't be silly. Of course it's okay.

BEN. I don't want to answer any more questions. I haven't done anything wrong.

NICHOLS. No one's saying you've done anything wrong, Ben.

BEN. Why can't I go to school then?

SOPHIE. You don't even like school!

BEN. I don't want him to ask me any more questions.

NICHOLS. Ben, I don't want to make you upset, but we have a few more questions we need to ask you to help us understand what happened on Monday night.

BEN. What don't you understand?

BEN *slides down in his chair.*

SOPHIE. Sit properly please.

BEN *slides further down.*

NICHOLS. How long have you been going next door to visit Daniel, can you remember when was the first time you went into the house?

BEN. No.

NICHOLS. You're eight, aren't you, Ben?

BEN. Yes.

NICHOLS. So was it before you were eight do you think?

BEN. Why do you want to know that?

NICHOLS. I'm just trying to understand your. I'm wondering how you and Daniel got to know each other.

BEN *starts kicking his feet on the chair.*

SOPHIE. Ben.

BEN. I don't know why I have to answer questions!

NICHOLS. To help me understand, Ben.

Pause.

Okay?

Pause.

Because an eight-year-old little boy doesn't normally decide to go out of his house in the middle of the night without telling his mum where he's going.

BEN. I did tell her.

NICHOLS. What do you mean?

BEN. I wrote it down.

NICHOLS. You wrote what down? Where did you write it down?

SOPHIE *visibly stiffens.*

Pause.

BEN. I wrote it on the blackboard.

NICHOLS. Where's the blackboard?

BEN. There.

Nothing on the board. It is freshly wiped.

I did write it. It got rubbed off.

SOPHIE *covers her face.*

I heard a scratching in the loft, it sounded like an orphan
from a children's home in the Victorian times. I thought
about what Daniel would do if he was scared, and then
I started wondering what he was doing, and then I thought
I'd rather be in his house, with him.

I came downstairs and wrote on the blackboard. I wrote that
I was going to go next door to see Daniel –

SOPHIE. I didn't see it, honestly, I didn't see it until last night.

BEN. I thought, what if he's scared too.

Because *his* mum had gone out as well.

Pause.

SOPHIE *closes her eyes momentarily. Then holds her head
high.*

NICHOLS. So am I right in thinking there was no adult in the
house on Monday night when Ben climbed out of his
bedroom window and went into your neighbour's house?

SOPHIE. I know this looks terrible.

NICHOLS. Your husband wasn't here, no? –

SOPHIE. No. / Of course not.

NICHOLS. And no babysitter, nothing like that? No. Okay.

SOPHIE. I assumed he was asleep obviously! I only meant to
pop out for a couple of minutes, I would never have gone out
if / I'd known he was awake.

NICHOLS. But you ended up being out for longer than that,
didn't you, Sophie?

SOPHIE *looks at* NICHOLS.

SOPHIE. Yes.

NICHOLS. You were pulled over at one thirteen on the Goose Green roundabout where you were asked to give the police a sample of breath to test for alcohol.

SOPHIE. And they wouldn't let me get back in the car!

Have you known the whole time?

NICHOLS. Just since this morning.

SOPHIE. What are you playing games with *me* for? Going through this ridiculous charade. What about him next door? / Taking advantage of the moment

NICHOLS. Our concerns still stand regarding Mr Angelis –

SOPHIE. Exactly! So, can we get back to that please?

This is a totally separate issue.

Shouldn't you be concentrating your efforts on finding out what kind of a man encourages a friendship with an eight-year-old boy, hanging out with him in the middle of the night, not thinking to let his parent know?

Instead of hauling me over the coals for a lapse in.

I haven't broken the law! It's not illegal to nip out and leave a child for five minutes. What's the real issue here? I'm a single mother with a young son living next door to a suspected paedophile.

BEN. Who?

SOPHIE. What are you actually doing about that?

NICHOLS. You didn't mention when you were pulled over that you had left a child alone at home?

SOPHIE. I had intended to nip out for *five* minutes, to get some cigarettes. Thanks to your colleagues accusing me of a whole load of made-up stuff and stopping me from getting back in my car, it ended up being, a bit longer than that.

Look. I don't have to answer your questions.

Obviously, it never occurred to me he might get up and go *out*.

Why would a child *do* that? He was fast asleep…

Pause.

It's not as if I don't feel terrible about it.

NICHOLS. I see.

SOPHIE. And I may lose my job, so. You win!

And then Simon will get hold of it, stoking up his case against me.

Pause.

She closes her eyes momentarily.

Why don't you carry on trying to find out what happened next door, that's the important thing surely –

Flash of lights up on PEPPY *sitting in* DANIEL*'s armchair in No. 23.*

JODY *is taking her photograph.*

JODY. Do you mind if we open these curtains, get a bit more light in perhaps.

PEPPY. Oh those curtains don't really open, I think they are having their last legs. Is my brother, when is Daniel coming home?

JODY. I don't know about any of that side of things I'm afraid.

PEPPY. Did they read his notebook? I gave it to the lady. I'm sorry it got a bit messed up, yes, he got very angry about the crossing-out, he likes to keep it in order I think, he's a very organised person normally, but yes, he just made a small mistake and had to, change a tiny. Yes because you can see it says, very clearly, that he told the next-door child, the disappeared boy, he couldn't come in to the house, so really he didn't disappear here because I was in York you see and he definitely put the chain on, this is what it says in the notebook.

PEPPY *runs out of breath. She looks vacant for a moment.*

She is having difficulty catching her breath.

JODY *takes a photograph of her.*

PEPPY *stares into the camera.*

When are you taking the photographs of the bedding?

JODY (*laughs, not understanding*). Nearly there.

JODY *takes another photograph.*

That's great, Penny, can you just tuck that stray hair behind your ear for me?

PEPPY *tucks her hair behind her ear and stares into the camera lens.*

PEPPY. Do you know when Daniel's coming home? Have I asked you that before? There are so many people, coming in and going out, I lose track of all the faces. You all have the same face!

JODY. Maybe you could call the station, ask to be put through to the custody suite?

PEPPY. I don't know the number, nobody told me the. What's the number?

JODY. I don't know, you should be able to google it.

PEPPY *stares blankly.*

JODY *takes her picture.*

There we go.

That's lovely.

Can I quickly use your loo?

PEPPY. Are you from Lewisham police station?

JODY *takes a couple of pictures of the room.*

JODY. Is it upstairs? The loo?

PEPPY. Are you The Forensics?

Pause.

JODY *puts her camera away.*

Why are you in my house?

JODY. Sorry, I thought this was all arranged, there's a new woman, on the news desk, I hate being put in this position.

PEPPY. Who are you?

JODY *gathers her stuff.*

PEPPY *sits very still, her hands folded in her lap and looking down.*

I don't know why you come into my house and take my portrait I do not think I would come into your house like this, I don't think so, no!

JODY. Yeah, sorry, listen, I'm done now anyway, I'll get out of your hair. Don't worry about the loo, I'll hold on. Cross my legs!

PEPPY. Maybe your picture will make me like *La Bella Nani*! This is a very important one, this painting, everyone says, 'Oh yes, the sophisticated lace work! Look, the velvet of her dress!' This shows us the Venetian fashions of the time, maybe 1536, 1546 perhaps.

But I don't say this, 'No, I say, who is she? Who is this lady with her hand like this on her chest.'

PEPPY *puts her hand on her chest lightly, exactly.*

With her hand very light here and her shy face. Who is this? Everywhere in the books, unknown identity, unknown identity. So, when I was a student at Trinity, I travelled to Paris, I went to the Louvre, and yes, there it was on the wall, unknown identity!

She is holding on to her soul I think, because Veronese is making a portrait and he will show it all over Italy. It will make a big splash! But she has no name! Just *La Bella Nani*, just this.

JODY. Well, I'm just doing my job, so.

PEPPY. Yes. Like Veronese, he was an artist.

JODY. Well, I wouldn't go that far!

Pause.

God, I feel bad now.

PEPPY. Yes I feel bad.

My brother Daniel feels bad too, I think. Everyone feels bad, this really is a very serious and terrible situation.

Pause.

Nevermind.

Lights fade.

Scene Four

No. 23.

Late afternoon.

SOPHIE *stands in the doorway, holding on to the door frame. She is shaky, she has had a drink, or two drinks, to give her the courage to come.*

PEPPY *is watching her from the kitchen. She is wearing a huge heavy piece of blue-velvet material wrapped around her like a shawl, and a string of pearls.*

SOPHIE. I came because.

I'm not at work, obviously. I phoned in, told them. I was going to work at home.

I don't seem to be able to. Concentrate.

Because. I had no idea about any of this. I thought he was asleep in bed, I had no idea he was here.

I keep going over and over it in my head, the police said Ben's been in here before. When? I mean, when? Did he come. Because, obviously, if I had had any idea that he was hanging around with.

SOPHIE*'s eyes dart round the room.*

I know what you're thinking, what kind of mother doesn't notice when her son slips out of the house in the middle of the night? Well.

I've had a lot going on lately.

We moved here to have a fresh start. Ha!

I don't know if you heard. I lost a baby. He was eleven weeks old and the policewoman had to prise him out of my arms to take him away.

Perhaps this is the rock bottom I need to hit before I can come back up. Fuck, who knows. It can't get much worse can it? When your eight-year-old son sneaks out of the house in the middle of the night to hang out with the paedo next door.

PEPPY (*all her strength*). My brother does not have the sounds in his head to make sense of the words you use. He is his own language, he won't understand you, there are no ways to explain your imaginings to him, he will never believe it is possible.

He is the kindest one you can ever meet, he is the king of kindness.

We were *born* in this house.

SOPHIE. Why is your brother so interested in my son?

PEPPY. I said to my brother, 'Do not open the door when this boy comes, do not let him in,' and what happens? He comes round to the back door, this door will not lock, the key is disappeared, we cannot keep him out.

SOPHIE. Oh come on, what would an eight-year-old want here?

PEPPY. You, people.

You do not know us, your eyes always looking down.

My brother is decency. He is goodness.

He has never known people who think the world is bad like you do. You want to spread poison from house to house until all people think bad things like you.

PEPPY *stands like a warrior, her arm across her body like a shield.*

My mother. My father. My uncle. My brother, Daniel Angelis, a good man. All my family, decent people. Always. Every time.

SOPHIE. If he's so decent, then what's he doing in a police cell? You're going to have to see what's in front of your face – if he was innocent they'd have sent him home by now, wouldn't they?

DANIEL walks into the doorway behind SOPHIE.

He has a plastic bag and his hair is parted differently.

PEPPY looks at DANIEL.

SOPHIE turns to look at him.

The three stand in silence for a moment.

PEPPY stands tall, her head held high.

SOPHIE loses her nerve. She looks down. She goes.

Pause.

DANIEL. I was going to get the 484 bus but the nine minutes past didn't come. I walked. The nineteen past went past me and the twenty-nine past went past me. I walked all the way. It took me thirty-six minutes.

PEPPY. Did you get lost?

DANIEL. No. I know the way.

PEPPY. Why didn't you get on the bus?

DANIEL. I like walking.

Pause.

PEPPY. Come in then.

DANIEL comes in. He doesn't look quite at home.

PEPPY closes the front door.

DANIEL takes his coat off. He is wearing his trousers with his pyjama top.

You've still got your pyjama top on.

DANIEL. I know.

PEPPY tuts.

DANIEL stands in the middle of the room.

PEPPY. I think someone could have rung me and told me you were on your way home, do you think, Daniel? Did you tell them to ring me? Didn't you ask them?

DANIEL. They said they would leave a message on your mobile phone.

PEPPY. What mobile phone? I haven't got a mobile phone.

DANIEL. I know.

I know the way. I like walking.

PEPPY (*upset*). I haven't got a mobile phone!

DANIEL. I know.

PEPPY. Did you tell them I haven't got a mobile phone?

DANIEL. No.

Pause.

You should get one.

DANIEL *looks around the room.*

It's nice outside.

PEPPY. I've been so worrying about you, I didn't sleep one minute all night. I was walking all round the streets, I had to go out because the police had to move everything round, I walked up and down up and down, I didn't know what was going to happen next.

Pause.

Well?

DANIEL. I had a shower.

PEPPY. No, Daniel. What did they say?

DANIEL. Karen Parry sat next to me. She had a brooch with five diamonds on it, three white ones and two blue ones. She said I was good at giving detailed information.

She said I made the police's job easy because I was clear and precise. She lives in Sevenoaks in Kent and she has her own parking space.

I told the truth except about you pretending about Uncle Mannie being in bed upstairs. But they didn't ask me about that so I never told them a lie.

PEPPY. What did they say to you, Daniel, I need to know all the things they said to you of course. Why are you making me ask you all the questions, why are you like this tortoise with no sense?

DANIEL. They said I was good at answering questions.

PEPPY. About what? What questions? I don't think you are good at answering my questions.

DANIEL. I answered all their questions on my own. Without any help.

PEPPY. Yes, yes. Quickly, Daniel, don't be a tortoise like this, please.

DANIEL. It's confidential. It was my interview. I don't have to tell you.

PEPPY. Daniel. Stop it. You know you must tell me. You cannot keep things from me, I know what you are thinking, even in the dark, remember? You know this.

DANIEL *doesn't say anything.*

Daniel.

Pause.

I think you are hungry.

DANIEL. I had a sandwich.

PEPPY. What sandwich?

DANIEL. Egg.

PEPPY. You don't like egg.

DANIEL. I do.

It was nice. It is my favourite sandwich.

PEPPY. Well.

DANIEL. You can get other buses you know, Peppy, not just the 484 and the 171. There are buses to other places. Holborn and Putney and Waterloo and London Bridge. Some of them with an N in the number just go at night. I think I might get those buses.

PEPPY. At night? What for?

DANIEL. You can get a train from London Bridge to Sevenoaks, there's three an hour. You can get a timetable with the times on, Karen Parry had one in her bag. I'd like to go to Sevenoaks.

PEPPY. Stop it, Daniel, you are not making any sense. You are tired and have eaten the wrong food.

DANIEL. I am going to get a British atlas and look up Sevenoaks.

PEPPY. You can do that tomorrow. Sit down.

He sits in his armchair.

That's right.

Do you want to listen to your music?

DANIEL. No.

PEPPY. Where's your notebook?

DANIEL. I've got a new notebook.

DANIEL *takes a jotter pad out of his bag.*

Karen Parry gave it to me. She got it out of a packet in a cupboard. It's a real notebook like the ones the police use.

PEPPY *watches him closely for a while.*

PEPPY. It looks a bit flimsy I think, not good quality, not good-quality paper really.

DANIEL *writes fast.*

Are you writing all about what's happened at the police station? Everything that the people said to you about the next-door child, yes, Daniel? Also you can put everything that you said to them as well. That's right, this is the right way to do it.

DANIEL *is writing.*

Is this what you are doing, Daniel? What I said?

DANIEL. No.

I am writing about getting a different bus. I am writing about when I go to Sevenoaks on the train from London Bridge Station. And when I go to Karen Parry's house to see the view from her kitchen. I'm going to paint it. I am writing about all the things that I am going to do.

PEPPY. No, Daniel, that is not what this book is for. You are doing it wrong.

DANIEL. It's my book. Shhh. I am concentrating.

PEPPY. This book is for everything that is the truth, remember, everything must be in the right order, listen to me, Daniel, where are your listening ears.

DANIEL. I'm going to go to WHSmiths soon, Peppy, to buy a new book. Very soon this book will be full.

Karen Parry has a laptop. You can look things up on it and write on it and listen to music on it. I want to get one. They are three hundred and seventy-nine pounds and ninety-nine pence in Argos.

DANIEL *writes fast.* PEPPY *watches anxiously.*

PEPPY. Daniel. What did they say to you about the next-door child?

DANIEL. I was released without charge. They said my case was NFA.

PEPPY. What? Speak properly, Daniel, what is this?

DANIEL. It means No Further Action. They went to Benjamin Banks' house and spoke to him. Then they said it was NFA.

PEPPY. Why has no one called to tell me this NFA?

Sit up properly, stop bending, what has happened to you, Daniel, you are different, not in a good way. What have people been saying to you?

DANIEL. Nothing.

PEPPY. Stop it.

DANIEL. Benjamin Banks told them I was his friend. I told you I was his friend but you didn't believe me.

PEPPY. And why is this? Because you are coming in saying things I don't know about, but you don't know how serious it is for me. Someone else is going to buy this house and live here with a German businessman. He's going to write a cheque!

DANIEL. Who?

PEPPY. Yes, now you listen! We have to move away because there are too many children here, Daniel, they will not like it if we live here, this is why the water is not coming in the tap, the hedge is too big for the pavement! They want us to go. They have taken photographs of the bedding. You never listen to me and look what has happened now. You have left a nasty taste in their mouths. What are we going to do? Everyone has disappeared, everything is changing, I want Uncle Mannie, Daniel, I don't know where he is.

DANIEL. I was thinking, I wonder if he's dead.

Pause.

PEPPY. What then? What will happen then?

DANIEL *makes an earnest declaration.*

DANIEL. I will look after you, Peppy. Let me.

PEPPY (*laughs*). You! What can you do? Haha! I am the eldest remember.

DANIEL. I can. Karen Parry said I can do more things than I think.

PEPPY. Karen Parry! Why am I hearing about only Karen Parry! Has Karen Parry been waiting while this house is full of people in paper clothes picking up and moving Mama and Father's precious things? No. I don't think so. I think they are not our things any more, Daniel, this is not our house. You are not my brother.

DANIEL. Yes I am.

PEPPY. No, Daniel.

The door opened and the whole world pushed in and touched everything in this house, making it all wrong. You did this, Daniel, and I don't think you are sorry. All you talk about is Karen Parry but where are the boy's pyjama bottoms?

DANIEL. What?

PEPPY. His mother wants them back, he only has half his pyjamas.

DANIEL. They were wet. He took them off and put them down.

He looks around on the floor.

PEPPY. No, Daniel, they are not here. This is very serious, Daniel, you are like some imbecile!

DANIEL. It's true. Karen Parry said I was good at telling the truth. You'd like Karen Parry, I know you would.

PEPPY (*with quiet malice*). You are causing trouble, Daniel, this is not how people do things.

DANIEL *doesn't say anything.*

PEPPY *goes over to the kitchen and turns her back on* DANIEL.

You are a numbskull. You are a halfwit, a birdbrain. Yes this is the truth.

What do you do for me? I do everything for you and I don't think you care about it. I came back here from university to look after you and you never say thank you. The life I left behind! I was really very happy in my room in Cambridge with my desk and the round patchwork cushion for my chair that Mama made, and the bedspread with little knots along the edges and the people in the kitchen, 'Hello, Penelope, good morning! Goodnight!' All the books in the library, you could read any books you liked and go there anytime in the day and in the night, I really was very happy there reading all the books – you could stay there one hundred years or two hundred years and still there would be new books to read. About Caravaggio and Titian; all these important painters and scholars. I could have been in a book like this in the library at the University of Cambridge! I dreamed about it! And they would say, 'Yes, I remember Penelope Angelis, she was a very good student, a very hard-working one.' Oh I miss all those books in the library! About all these whole people who did not have to turn away from their studies to come home and look after their birdbrain brother Daniel, I am sorry to say this but it is true. I abandoned a big opportunity to look after you, Daniel, there was a life that I hadn't started to live in even, I had stood at the gate and looked in and seen what it would be like. I had to leave it there, empty without me inside it. Who is going to put a picture of me in a book in the library at the University of Cambridge? No one, Daniel, because of you. And are you grateful? No.

DANIEL *sits quietly for a moment, thinking about this.*

DANIEL. Why did you leave Cambridge University?

PEPPY. To look after you, why have you not been listening to me, I'm saying all this to you, what do you mean 'Why?' Why? This is what I'm talking about! You have big ears that you never use.

DANIEL. The bedspread with the knots along the edges wasn't on your bed in Cambridge University, it was in the hospital, Peppy.

Pause.

PEPPY. No, Daniel, you are remembering wrong.

DANIEL. No, I'm not.

Me and Uncle Mannie came to visit you. You sat next to the window with the knot blanket over your legs, the blanket was folded. Someone had brushed your hair flat. We were going to take you out in Uncle Mannie's car, it was a plan, but you didn't want to come. You didn't want to speak to us. You kept trying to take your bandages off. The nurse gave me some bread and I fed the birds in the garden, it had mould on it, I can remember.

PEPPY. Mama said when there are two children, one is always the watcher, and one the dancer. She said, 'You are the dancer, Peppy.' Mama said it was me, but still, I had to leave it all behind to look after you.

DANIEL. Mama died.

PEPPY. Yes, before she died she told me this I mean. Then I had to leave everything in Cambridge to look after you. Yes.

Pause.

DANIEL. When Mama died she told me to look after *you*, Peppy.

PEPPY. No, Daniel. (*Starts to cry, tries not to.*)

DANIEL. She did.

PEPPY. What are you saying this nonsense for? No this is not right. Why are you lying?

DANIEL (*gently*). It was because of the voices in your head and the hospital.

PEPPY. It was not a hospital, no, no, you are remembering wrong, Daniel, because you are too tired. The knot blanket was definitely in my room at my college in the Cambridge University. Go to bed please. Tomorrow we will be back to normal I think.

DANIEL. What if I am the dancer?

PEPPY. No, Daniel, I don't think so. I am the dancer, Mama told me. Go to bed.

DANIEL. Can we both be the dancer? I don't want to be the watcher.

PEPPY. No, Daniel. This is not how it works.

DANIEL *looks at* PEPPY. *He looks as if he will say something but then decides not to. After a moment* DANIEL *sits down in the armchair, he waits a moment before putting his headphones on and pressing play on the tape recorder.*

PEPPY *goes to the back door and opens it.*

Stands in the door way and calls out into the garden.

Charlie Brown! Charlie Brown!

I don't know where he is, he is always nearby until today. By my side always. Suddenly now I think he has been squashed by a big fast car. I think he has been stabbed in New Cross Gate.

(*Vicious*.) Look, Daniel, look what you have done!

Pause.

I read your notebook, Daniel. I know what you did.

PEPPY *turns. She sees that* DANIEL *has put his headphones on.*

She lurches towards him, she stumbles, tripping over as if her legs give way suddenly. She gets up and grabs the headphones off DANIEL*'s ears, screaming in his face.*

I KNOW WHAT YOU DID!

PEPPY *starts to attack him, pummelling his face and chest. He holds her off easily, he stands, they fall into the piles of things surrounding them.*

DANIEL. Stop it, Peppy, the neighbours will hear you.

PEPPY (*crying, still fighting but losing strength*). Why did you let me go all the way to York on the Megabus, Daniel? Why? You knew Uncle Mannie would not be in his house, you knew he wouldn't come for Christmas, Daniel, you KNEW. Why did you let me go all that way on my own, Daniel?

DANIEL (*upset*). I don't know.

PEPPY. Why did you open the letter, Daniel, I open the letters, I am the eldest.

DANIEL. I open letters, Peppy, sometimes I get up earlier than you and I open them.

PEPPY. This was a very important letter, Daniel, you should not have opened it and if you opened it by mistake you should have closed it again and stuck it back with Sellotape and put it back on the floor by the letter box for me to open. This letter came in February, Daniel, this is very long for a secret from your sister, this is a very bad way to behave, this is not how people do things. This is a LIE, Daniel.

DANIEL. No it's not a lie, / it's not.

PEPPY. If you don't tell a person that someone that they love
has died, Daniel, this is the same as a lie.

Pause.

I think you know this.

DANIEL *doesn't say anything.*

PEPPY *is slowing down, running out of ammunition,
tripping over her words.*

An omission of truth is like a lie, Daniel, and I think, yes,
this is a bad one. Because, I went all the way to York by
myself and when I was gone you disappeared a child, Daniel,
and it is the last straw I am afraid. Maybe you should go and
live somewhere else, Daniel, maybe this is the best plan to
do, because I am too tired. I am too tired from looking after
you, really this is the truth.

Silence.

DANIEL. Have you taken your tablets today, Peppy?

PEPPY *doesn't look at him.*

DANIEL *goes to a drawer in the kitchen and gets a plastic
bag containing boxes of pills. He turns the tap on, it trickles
weakly into a cup. He waits patiently and then takes it to her
with the pills.*

DANIEL *helps* PEPPY *into the chair.*

DANIEL *stands next to the chair and patiently gives* PEPPY
her pills. She takes four.

DANIEL *pulls some velvet material over* PEPPY*'s knees and
tucks her in.*

Go to sleep, Peppy.

PEPPY. How can I go to sleep?

DANIEL. Do you want me to sing to you?

PEPPY. No definitely no.

PEPPY*'s eyes start to close.*

Make the drum on Charlie Brown's plate please, Daniel, stand at the back door and do it. He will hear it and come I think.

DANIEL *makes his way to the kitchen and finds a spoon and a plate and bangs it loudly.*

(*Calls out*.) Charlie Brown!

PEPPY *suddenly cries, big waves of grief come.*

Charlie Brown!

Mama!

Uncle Mannie!

Where are you?

Come back!

DANIEL *bangs the plate.*

Lights fade.

Scene Five

Eight weeks later.

The sound of a sewing machine, stopping and starting erratically.

The living room of No. 23 is taken over by the making of bunting. Great lengths of it tangle over the teetering piles of papers and books.

There are overflowing bags of old clothes with triangles cut out of them strewn around the room

DANIEL *sits in the middle of it with his big red headphones on, listening to a tape.*

PEPPY *is in good spirits. She sits at the table sewing on an ancient sewing machine.*

PEPPY *sews in the erratic way you might expect.*

PEPPY. This machine is very good, it is very easy to use, when Mama made our clothes she said the machine was slow and made always mistakes but I think this machine is really very good.

Do you remember, Daniel, the shirt Mama made you for Didi's christening?

She laughs heartily and looks at DANIEL. DANIEL *is listening to his tape.*

He can't hear me.

Daniel! Daniel!

DANIEL *looks up.* PEPPY *mimes removing his headphones. He takes them off.*

Do you remember the shirt Mama made for you with the big yellow collar?

DANIEL. No.

PEPPY *laughs.*

PEPPY. I think you do because you remember everything.

DANIEL *goes to put his headphones back on again.*

No, no, Daniel. We have lots of work to do you cannot just sit listening to tapes and not join in please.

DANIEL. What do I have to do? I don't want to.

PEPPY. You don't know what it is! Look! I am talking all about the sunshine shirt with the collar for Didi's christening, see here it is, on the flag here.

PEPPY *holds up a yellow triangle of fabric.*

Then another one further along.

And this one, what is this, do you remember?

DANIEL. Yes.

PEPPY. What is it?

DANIEL. My gardening trousers.

PEPPY. Yes! Why do you never go in the garden any more, Daniel? You should!

DANIEL. You cut up my trousers and put them on a flag.

PEPPY. You could plant some crocuses and sweetpeas and hollyhocks. This is a very good game, Daniel, Karen says it helps you to remember everything before you throw it away.

This is the dress I wore every time at church, and this is not very bright, not good for a flag really, just my school dress, the summer one, it is very faded and dull. And the cover of the cushions from the chair in Mama and Baba's room, the bedspread, the curtain from the front door in Grandma's house, what is this, I don't know, nothing, and this is Mama's skirt with the birds, where's a bird? Here it is, and another one with no head! Oh dear this is not good cutting! (*Laughs.*)

I think sewing is a very relaxing pastime, Daniel! I really do feel very relaxed. And do you know what I am thinking about when I am sewing? Do you know?

DANIEL *puts his headphones on,* PEPPY *doesn't notice.*

I am thinking about my namesake. Penelope. Because you know that Penelope was the Queen of Ithaca, don't you, Daniel. She was the wife of King Odysseus, Odysseus the Cunning he was called this as well, and he left Penelope to go to the Trojan War. And she waited to see him again, really a very long time, she was very patient, because the war was ten years long and his journey home, the same, another ten years! Imagine this! Suitors flocked to the palace, 'Marry me Penelope, marry me!' 'Your husband is gone for ever!' They wanted the throne of Ithaca, not really Penelope, these were very bad men. And Penelope said, no, I will not get married again until I finish these clothes I am weaving.

She was weaving, I am sewing, it is different, but I am thinking about her anyway.

But the big secret that nobody knew, was that every night she was undoing the weaving! She was destroying the clothes! Yes! Because she didn't want to get married to anyone else, she was longing and hoping that Odysseus would return for her. Ha! (*Laughs.*)

So you see, Daniel, Penelope is the name for a very loyal and faithful woman who does everything for her family.

DANIEL (*takes his headphones off*). Is it lunchtime?

PEPPY. We are having lunch in the garden today, I told you. Karen is coming and we are having a picnic lunch in the garden in the space that is there because I have thrown away some of Daddy's wood.

DANIEL. I don't want to have my lunch outside.

PEPPY. I know.

DANIEL. You said we didn't have to do it. You said no one had to do anything they didn't want to do.

PEPPY. Yes. That's right. You have free choice.

DANIEL. I am my own person.

PEPPY. I know. But remember Karen's husband is coming.

DANIEL. Laurence Parry?

PEPPY. Yes.

DANIEL. What for?

PEPPY. He is going to fix the tap. I told you. You don't listen to me, Daniel. You should go to SpecSavers to get a hearing aid I think, like Bill Oddie.

DANIEL *doesn't say anything.*

You can have your lunch inside, Daniel, and then come outside if you want to, it's up to you. It is your free choice.

DANIEL. I don't want to.

PEPPY. Karen is really very nice I think. Very kind.

PEPPY *rifles through a bag of clothes by her feet, she pulls things out and looks at them.*

What is this? (*Laughs.*) I don't know!

PEPPY *takes the scissors and cuts a triangular flag.*

PEPPY *carefully turns over one edge and pins it as she speaks.*

Maybe all the suitors that came to ask Penelope were not bad. Maybe some were good and wanted to make her happy. Because I think people are kind really, Daniel, I think so. I think it's less than four per cent, three per cent maybe. Maybe something like three-and-a-half per cent, Daniel, these people are not good. Not so good really. A small amount of people, sometimes with very loud voices! But very small amounts.

DANIEL. Paris stole Helen from Menelaus and he was the King of Sparta.

PEPPY. Yes. But I am talking about Penelope, Daniel, Penelope was the Queen of Ithaca. I am not talking about Helen and these other people.

(*Stops, checks herself.*) But this is very interesting, Daniel. This completely different thing that you are saying.

PEPPY *looks at* DANIEL, *she is smiling and nodding*.

But when I am sewing I think of Penelope. Penelope is the weaver, it means weaver. Peno is unfold. Lepo, is unroll. This is like weaving, working with material is like this. It is very relaxing.

DANIEL. What is 'Daniel'?

PEPPY. You know this, Daniel, why are you asking me this?

DANIEL. Say what it is.

PEPPY. 'God is my judge.'

DANIEL. Yes. That's right.

PEPPY. Why do you ask me these questions when you know the answers? You are always doing this.

DANIEL. I like it.

PEPPY. I know you do. You will make me go mad.

PEPPY *sews*.

There is a gentle knock on the front door and someone lets themselves in with a key.

KAREN*'s voice calls, 'Hello!'*

Who is it? Yes! Hello! Hello, Karen!

She looks at DANIEL.

Yes come in please!

KAREN *enters. She is carrying a flan with a tea towel over it.*

KAREN. You look busy! How are you getting on?

PEPPY. Yes, we are very busy. Daniel is very busy too.

KAREN (*looks at the bunting*). My goodness, you've done loads of it! And something smells good.

PEPPY *jumps up.*

PEPPY. Oh my walnut spice cake!

PEPPY *runs to the oven and opens the door. She takes out a cake.*

KAREN *puts down her flan and goes to look.*

KAREN. Mmmmm.

PEPPY. This is a very special cake, oh it looks like a very good one!

This is really a cake for Christmas time, but, I think you are allowed to have it another time as well.

KAREN. Oh yes, we don't need to tell anyone!

LAURENCE *enters carrying a bag for life and a tool bag.*

LAURENCE. Hello. I'm Laurence.

PEPPY *and* DANIEL *don't say anything,*

KAREN. Before you come in here you have to promise Peppy on your life that you won't tell anyone that this cake is meant to be eaten at Christmas.

LAURENCE. You what?

KAREN. I think we can trust him.

PEPPY. No, tell them it is Christmas! We can pretend it is Christmas. We can have Christmas any time we like. It is our own free choice.

PEPPY *transfers the cake on to a plate.*

She is pleased with it.

LAURENCE. What am I doing with this bag?

KAREN. Putting it in the garden please. It's for our picnic.

LAURENCE. Right.

> LAURENCE *takes the bag into the garden.*

PEPPY. I think Uncle Mannie would like this cake.

> KAREN *puts her hand on* PEPPY*'s arm briefly.*

KAREN. Oh, he would have loved it. We'll eat it in his honour. How's your sorting going? Show me the bag to go out.

> PEPPY *rushes over to a large bag by the sewing machine with some remnants of material in it.*

> LAURENCE *re-enters.*

LAURENCE. Did I lock the car?

KAREN. I don't know, did you?

LAURENCE. I'm going to check.

KAREN. Leave the door on the latch.

> LAURENCE *exits through the front.*

PEPPY. Here it is.

> KAREN *looks at* PEPPY*'s bag of remnants.*

KAREN. Not bad, not quite as good as yesterday though, are you slowing down a bit?

PEPPY. No I think I am still fast.

KAREN. No rush I suppose, you're taking it at your own pace, that's fine. As long as you're moving forward every day. Did you do the newspapers in the front room?

PEPPY. Not yet I think I will do this tomorrow.

KAREN. Are you still asking yourself the questions? Don't forget the questions, will you.

PEPPY. I do ask myself always, don't I, Daniel?

DANIEL. Yes.

PEPPY. Do I use this? Have I used this in the last three months? Does this bring beauty into my life? Oh dear!

Laughs and shakes her head.

He doesn't like it. It is driving him round the wall!

KAREN. Oh dear. (*Laughs.*) Well, I honestly do think the questions help.

PEPPY. Yes this is true.

KAREN. You'll like it when there's a bit more space for your painting though, won't you, Daniel? That front room's going to be your studio remember, you've got to be able to get in it.

PEPPY *picks up a plate and spoon and starts banging them together.*

PEPPY (*calls*). Charlie Brown! Charlie Brown!

LAURENCE *returns and goes to the sink.*

KAREN. All locked up now?

LAURENCE. I'd locked it!

They laugh. LAURENCE *sorts out his tools.*

LAURENCE. I'll have a go at that hedge when I've finished in here, hanging right over the pavement it is.

PEPPY. I do not want this cat in the garden at the picnic, I think he will be very afraid of all the noise and so I must shut him in here with Daniel.

KAREN. Aren't you coming to the picnic, Daniel?

PEPPY. No, Daniel is going to stay here and look after Charlie Brown, he is really very okay and fine, aren't you, Daniel?

KAREN. Oh that's a shame.

DANIEL (*to* PEPPY). What will I have for my lunch?

KAREN. Oh there's plenty of food –

PEPPY. You can have a piece of walnut spice cake, you would like this very much I think, can you remember how it tastes?

DANIEL. Yes. (*He doesn't like it*.)

KAREN. And you can always change your mind and come out and join us, can't you?

DANIEL *doesn't say anything.*

KAREN *and* PEPPY *work in the kitchen.* PEPPY *has half an onion that she is putting into a plastic bag, then into another plastic bag.* KAREN *watches her.*

Do you think you need to put that onion in more than one plastic bag?

PEPPY (*laughs*). I don't know what I'm doing!

KAREN. One bag's probably enough. In fact we could probably get rid of a few of these bags, what do you think?

PEPPY. Oh! (*Not sure*.) Yes okay maybe just one I think maybe.

PEPPY *watches anxiously as* KAREN *collects up some bags.*

KAREN. Right, so are we going to have this beautiful bunting at our picnic then?

PEPPY. Yes I will put it round the tree.

KAREN. Good idea.

LAURENCE. I'm going to get on with this first then, is that the plan?

KAREN. Yes that's right.

KAREN *washes her hands in the thin trickle of water and* LAURENCE *watches.*

They speak to each other.

You see, that's not right, is it?

LAURENCE. Well I know that, that's why I'm here, aren't I. Move out the way then and I'll get stuck in.

KAREN. Where's your sharp knives, Peppy?

PEPPY. Oh. Yes.

PEPPY *starts to open drawers and cupboards.*

LAURENCE. You going to do me in, are you?

KAREN (*laughing*). Well I will if you don't get on with sorting that tap yes! No, it's for my flan, isn't it!

KAREN *finds what she needs, she is very at home in the kitchen.*

LAURENCE *opens the cupboard under the sink. It's extraordinarily full.*

LAURENCE. Good Lord!

KAREN *gives him a stern look to silence him.*

She helps him empty it out.

PEPPY *gathers up the bunting and cuts it free from the machine.*

They all work in silence for a while.

DANIEL *watches* PEPPY.

PEPPY. What do you think Mama would say, Daniel. If she saw the flags with all the clothes and cushions flying over our garden! She would be so surprised I think, what would she say?

DANIEL. I think she would say, 'Don't do that, Peppy, take it down.'

PEPPY (*laughing*). No! She would be happy, she would be proud, it looks like a big celebration, she always liked celebrations and things like this, don't you remember. Oh yes, I think she would be very happy to see these flags.

They are bringing beauty into our life.

KAREN. Come on then, the app on my phone said there's a sixty per cent chance of rain at two o'clock so we've got an hour of sunshine to get this picnic eaten.

PEPPY *collects the bunting together and moves towards the back door.*

Oh Peppy, you've upstaged me with your beautiful cake and all this bunting. Aren't you clever.

KAREN *takes her flan outside.*

My boring old flan.

(*From outside.*) There's a bit of an edge to this wind, you might need a coat actually, Peppy.

LAURENCE *lies down on the floor in the cupboard under the sink.*

PEPPY *puts her coat on.*

At the door PEPPY *stops.*

PEPPY. Are you going to be all right, Daniel?

DANIEL. Don't leave me, Peppy, promise me.

PEPPY. I am only outside this back door, I will eat my lunch and look at the flags and then come back inside, I won't leave you, of course not.

Silly donkey.

PEPPY *turns to go to the garden, she has a triangle cut out of the back of her coat.*

We can hear KAREN *and* PEPPY *talking in the garden about how much wood used to be there and how much nicer it is with some space to sit in.* KAREN *is being really positive about it all.*

After a moment, BEN *comes into the hall and stands in the doorway.*

BEN. Hello.

How come your front door's open?

DANIEL. You're not allowed in here.

BEN. I know, but it's okay because the door's open.

Pause.

I'm moving on Wednesday.

DANIEL. I know.

BEN. How do you know?

DANIEL. Karen Parry told me.

BEN. Who?

DANIEL. My support worker.

BEN. Oh. Okay.

Pause.

DANIEL. You're not allowed in here without an adult.

BEN. I know, you just said that.

Pause. He stays there.

My mum said I could give you these.

DANIEL. What?

BEN. They're just some envelopes with my new address, my mum stuck stamps on already. There's five of them. You can write to me if you want.

DANIEL *doesn't say anything.*

So do you want to write to me?

DANIEL. Yes.

BEN. Cool.

BEN *puts the envelopes down on* DANIEL'*s table, then he goes back to the doorway.*

Oh yeah, in 1672 the Dutch killed and ate their prime minister, can you believe it?

DANIEL. Go back to your house. They'll dial 999 and call the police.

BEN. Okay.

Well, I'm moving on Wednesday.

DANIEL. I know.

DANIEL *puts his headphones on and picks up his notebook.*

BEN *stays in the doorway for a little while, then he exits.*

DANIEL *inspects the envelopes and makes a note in his book.*

After a while LAURENCE *gets up.* DANIEL *had not realised he was there, he looks panicked.*

LAURENCE *turns on the tap.*

The water flows perfectly.

LAURENCE. Hey presto!

LAURENCE *smiles at* DANIEL.

Lights slow fade to black.

The End.

www.nickhernbooks.co.uk

facebook.com/nickhernbooks

twitter.com/nickhernbooks